To Br

a lifelong friend (and a ya
who knows where all
the bodies are buried.
God Bless You!
JOE McCORMICK

Redneck In Paris

11-25-2018

Redneck In Paris

A Book of Short Stories

By Joe McCormick

Big Springs Press

2018

Redneck In Paris by Joe McCormick

Cover design and cover art: Joe McCormick

Publisher: Big Springs Press, Pinson TN 38366

Copy Editor: Cindy Rubin

Production Editor: Missy Frazier

ISBN: 978-1-387-91833-1

10 9 8 7 6 5 4 3 2 1

1. Fiction 2. Humor 3. Christian 4. Biblical Humor

Printed in the USA

Books may be purchased by contacting the publisher, Big Springs Press, at 676 Cedarfield Rd, Pinson TN 38366; or at

www. JoeMcCormickCountry.com

This is a work of humor. It is a compilation of stories based on actual events, complete fiction, and everything in between. Other than "The Beloved Pastor of Pinson", all the stories have elements that have been embellished or modified to suit the storytelling style of the author. Many of the people are real people in the author's life who have been shown in humorous light, and most certainly with no malicious intent. Most of the events actually happened but are retold here from the author's twisted and humorous point of view. Please enjoy.

Dedicated to David Olhausen

Why I Write

I have always liked stories. My mother used to read to us when she put us to bed at night. Our favorite book was about the adventures of an old gentleman rabbit named Uncle Wiggly. Each night he would escape from one peril only to be threatened with calamity again by the end of the story, leaving us hungry to hear the next installment, which we had to wait until the following night to hear.

Growing up, I read voraciously, from comic books to the classics, and began early to try to write my own stories. My first attempt at serious writing was a series of humorous tales from my childhood, a little collection I put in a binder and gave to my mother as a Christmas gift. I still have many of those stories, some of which are included here. You will recognize which stories are true and which are what I call "drivel," but I hope you will find them all to be entertaining and edifying.

I write simply because there are things I want to say, and to share with others, and I have found no better way to express myself than by writing. It gives me time to develop my thoughts and to present them without interruption. There may be long pauses in writing, but the reader does not see them. In the final analysis, I think that if I could find no other reason to write, I would do it simply because I find it to be altogether pleasant and joyful, and immensely satisfying.

My sincere hope is that the reader will find the same satisfaction.

-Joe McCormick

Table of Contents

Preface (Why I Write)

It Happened!

(Almost) Biblical

IT HAPPENED !

Shot Day

Cruelly, it had been announced in advance, giving me a couple of extra days to sweat. When Miss Moselle Jones, teacher of the one room school at County Line, first gave us the news it meant nothing to me. I didn't know what "inoculation" meant. I couldn't even pronounce "vaccination." But when they told me in plain Tennessee English that it meant a doctor was going to come there and give me a shot, my knees turned to water. In my entire eight-year career as a human person I never remembered anyone giving me a shot in my body before.

Finally, the day had come, and here I stood waiting my turn in the hot midday sun, shaking like there was three feet of snow on the ground. I felt like an old man.

Preparations had been well made. You'd think the Chester County Health Department would overlook a little hayseed one room school back in the woods on the county line, but no – they sent in their top string. Shaky old Doc Steadman and a goofy looking buck-toothed nurse set them up a table outside in the

1

shade of a grove of trees. Poles had been cut and nailed to the trees on either side, like handrails, or more like a loading chute, to make a lane leading up to the table. Every kid in school, grades one through eight, was herded into that chute, where he was supposed to stand quietly in line and await - with joy - his turn.

And there by the table at the other end of the line sat cheerful old Doc Steadman in a rickety cane bottom chair, glasses sliding off the end of his sweaty nose. The doc's bright little eyes peered impishly at us over the edge of those glasses, and he showed his store-bought teeth in what seemed to me to be the most diabolical grin I ever saw. It gave me the creeps. In one bony, shaky hand he held the biggest, meanest, poisonest shot-giving thing that had ever been made.

My confidence in doctors evaporated right out of the pores of my skin. I didn't have to wait to read it in the newspapers to find out if it was time to leave out of there or not.

I hawed, and bumped into the rail on my left. Then I tried to gee, and ran into the other rail. So, I commenced whoa-backing... but mama had me blocked. She'd been smart enough to stand behind me in that line, and now she clamped a hand on each of my trembling shoulders to keep me from bolting. Biting my lip, I had to stand there and watch what happened to the victims before me. But I kept my feet in gear.

Doc Steadman had already stuck a couple of the kids, and they walked off like nothing much had happened. One little girl had a tear in her eye, but so far things were going along without a hitch.

The Doc kept up a running chatter as he worked.

"A nurse taught me how to do this here," he would say, as he snatched a little brown arm, shoved the needle in and shired down on the plunger. His hands shook so badly I kept waiting to see if he'd miss and stick the needle in the back of his own hand. He didn't though.

After he squirted the juice in, the Doc would yank the needle out, push his glasses back up on his beak and reload. In those days they didn't have disposable syringes and needles. They had to unscrew the used needle and drop it in a pan of antiseptic solution, then they'd take a new needle out of another tray and screw it onto the syringe.

Well, the old Doc managed to botch it just about every time. The nurse usually had to take over and straighten things out for him. That was supposed to be the nurse's job anyway, but the Doc was having fun putting on a show for all us kids. Probably the first time they'd let the old coot out of the office all year.

Doc picked up a little bottle of medicine and tried to unscrew the cap. It wouldn't budge. "Nurse showed me how to open a bottle like this here," he chuckled, tapping the bottle upside-down on the table. He strained unsuccessfully at the cap again. The nurse took the bottle from his hand, slipped the cap off with a dainty twist, and handed it back to him without a word. Never interrupting his chatter, the Doc crammed the needle down through the rubber stopper of the bottle and sucked up a syringe full of the evil looking medicine. He put a slight pressure on the plunger and squirted a few drops out on the ground. Then, pushing his bifocals back into position, he made a grab for the next customer.

Benny Moore was standing right in front of me. We called him "Sack" Moore because he always had a sack of Bull Durham tobacco in the bib pocket of his overalls. Benny was a tall, lanky boy. His hair stuck out stiff at the back of his head, like a porcupine. But we all knew that ol' Benny was afraid of nothing.

When it came his turn ol' Sack squared around and strutted right on up to the Doc with a cocky grin on his mug, rolling up his sleeve. His confidence seemed to crack a mite when the old Doc made a grab for his arm and missed, snagging a gallus instead.

Doc never missed with that needle, though. He r'ared back and jobbed it in all the way to the bone in Benny Moore's skinny arm.

Benny's scream made my hair stand on end.

The rocket scientists from NASA should have been there that day to see old Doc Steadman launch Benny Moore. They might have learned a thing or two about how to put an object into orbit from a flat-footed start.

It seems that with his arthritic old hands Doc had not got the needle screwed down tight enough, and when ol' Benny flinched, why, the needle broke right off in his arm. Benny naturally called the hogs all the way to Afghanistan and hauled off and jumped higher than I would have believed a human could jump. The first limb on the tree he was under looked to be about twenty feet high. It would not have been a great exaggeration to say that Benny missed it completely on the way up, but it broke his fall some on the way down.

Doc Steadman's glasses flew off his nose, and the goofy buck-toothed nurse fell backward. Benny was flying around knocking things over, holding his arm right below where the needle was sticking out, squalling like a turpentined cat in a hip boot. His screams could have flaked the paint off the schoolhouse wall. It was quite a show.

All eyes were on Benny as he bounded down the hill and disappeared into the distance, galloping barefooted down the gravel road toward his home. Everyone kept staring in the direction ol' Sack had gone, until they could no longer hear his blood-curdling cries.

In the dead silence following the fireworks, my mama suddenly came out of her trance and remembered the business at hand. She went to push me forward to get my shot, but her hands met empty air. Startled, she looked around in amazement. I was nowhere to be seen! Why – I had just been standing there a split second ago with her hands on my shoulders. She could still feel the sweat I'd left on her fingers. But the only sign she found that I'd been there was two barefoot pug marks where I had whirled and dug off low and fast, firing myself like a cannon shot right between Mama's legs. I was around the corner of the schoolhouse and out of sight quicker than a gallon of mineral oil can go through a constipated mule.

Even as Mama turned I was already deep in the woods, threshing through the underbrush, clawing through briar thickets and poison oak, conscious of no sensation except terror – an overpowering horror of a gigantic nightmare needle that surely must be in hot pursuit of me, oozing ugly green slime.

My uncle Ben was the one who found me, torn and bleeding from multiple scratches, hiding under a bed on our screened in back porch. They had already searched everywhere else in the house, with me trembling at every footstep I heard. I was afraid if they found me they would haul me back up there to the schoolhouse and let old Doc Steadman use me for target practice.

Uncle Ben must have heard my teeth chattering. I saw his feet come into view and stop beside the bed. He pulled up the bedspread and his grinning face appeared.

"You better come on out from under there, boy," he said.

"Is that there doctor still up there with that dang needle?" I said.

Only after Ben assured me that the doctor and nurse had already packed their gear and returned to Henderson, and Shot Day was officially over, did I breathe a great sigh of relief and crawl out from under that bed.

Since that time, I have been in places of danger and done things that haven't produced anything approaching the kind of fear Old Doc Steadman inspired in me the day he lost the needle in ol' Sack Moore. I have picked fights with people bigger than me, had car wrecks, been in airports in foreign countries where they frisk you by hand while a guard holding a machinegun stands by. I even got married. In none of these things did I show more than the normal amount of fear and trepidation. There even came a time when I could stand to take a shot.

But you will search my body in vain looking for that little round scar that most people show as evidence that they have had their "school shots."

Maybe I was inoculated by fear. Anyway, I never got any of those diseases.

The Onions

More than once when I was a kid, funny books kept me from being all that I know I should have been.

One day I was reading one of the devilish things when my Mama interrupted my vicarious adventure. She told me to go out in the garden and get some onions for dinner.

"Uh – huh," I mumbled. But I was just coming to the part where Ol' Roy was tied up by the rustlers and left in a gully for a flash flood to wipe him out. So, I read on to the next page.

"...And be sure you pull every other one, so you won't thin them out too much," Mama was saying. That much my conscious mind registered. *Wait, hold on a minute! There comes Trigger, and he's working on the ropes with his teeth...but the wall of water is only five feet away!*

"I said NOW!"

The funny book went straight up, and I went out the back door too fast for anything hard and painful to hit me. The screen door banged shut behind me. Ol' Roy would just have to get out of his fix the best way he could without me. A man had to take time out to do his work every once in a while.

We had a fine stand of onions in that garden, all thick and green and a foot high. As I waded in I tried to remember what Mama's orders had been. Let's see now...didn't she say something about pulling up every other one? So, I set to work. The sun was warm on my shoulders, and my mind slipped easily back into thoughts of cowboys and Indians and rustlers and horses, until there I was, straightening up at the end of the row...and I had one heck of an armload of onions. Staggering up the porch steps with my burden, I wondered what in the world Mama was planning to do with so many onions. But mine not to reason why...

Somehow, when I dumped those onions on the kitchen table and saw the look on Mama's face – I knew I was in trouble.

At first, she was speechless when she saw that mountain of onions I held in both arms, like a pile of firewood. Then she found her voice, and it cut like a switch. "Boy, didn't you hear me when I told you to go down that row and pull every other onion *until you had enough for dinner?*"

"Well, uh..." There wasn't a lot I could say. It wouldn't have helped anyway.

Now, at this point, your average mean old mama would have taken a stick and beaten the garden dust out of her darling

9

little boy, just to make sure he paid attention the next time. But not my Mama. No sirree! My Mama was more progressive than that. She believed in fitting the punishment to the crime. She handed me a paring knife and a big white bowl. Then she pulled a chair out for me and pointed to the pile of onions. "Get busy," was all she said.

Twenty minutes later I had those onions peeled and washed, the bowl rounded full. Then Mama showed her vicious streak.

"Now, young man," she said, "you set right there, and don't you get up until you *eat every one of them onions!"*

I couldn't believe it. My heart hit the bottom of my belly. Why – Hitler wouldn't have said something like that to the Jews! If I had known anything about that rapture they talk about in the Bible I would have prayed for it to come right then and there. But I saw I had gotten myself into a fix that there was only one way out of, so I just swallowed a couple of times and set to.

Pretty soon I had tears and onion juice all over my face. Truth to tell, I didn't really eat every one of those onions, though it is sometimes told on me that I did. I had hardly eaten more than half a gallon, which was maybe two-thirds of the bowl, before I caught Mama's head turned and threw the rest out the window. I sometimes suspect that Mama saw that I was turning as green as those onions, and out of mercy turned her head on purpose to give me a chance to get off the hook. I do remember the strange way she was shaking, like a person will do when they laugh, but her face was still all scowly and mean looking.

Anyway, I learned at least two lessons from that little episode. I learned that if a kid didn't listen when his mama speaks, he might have to bite off more than he can chew. I also learned not to put no trust in friends, for they all failed me after that. Though I washed every day and brushed my teeth regular with sody and salt, for at least a week after eating all those onions I was the loneliest kid in school.

Stick Fighting

Along about my twelfth year, I read a book about Robin Hood, and it was a great influence on me. My brothers could see the difference in the way I acted as soon as we got off the school bus in front of our house at Five Points every afternoon. I had quit carrying around a cap pistol and had gone out in the woods and cut me a long pole to carry around. I was thinking of myself as Robin Hood now, instead of Roy Rogers or Gene Autry. My ignorant brothers laughed at me for toting around a long pole and taking a swing at every stationary object from an old crate out in the yard to the side of the house. I heard Jerry remark to Mama one night that I had just about knocked all the dead limbs off the trees in the woods behind our house. Mama was used to the dumb things her three boys were always doing, and she didn't even raise an eyebrow. But I could tell that Jerry and Mick thought I had a bulb loose because I was out every afternoon whaling away at dead limbs with that dumb stick. I'm sure it caused a single question to arise in their minds: Why?

My brothers had obviously never read about Robin Hood. Had they done so, they would know that the pole I was wielding was not a "stick." It was a regulation size quarterstaff, just like in the book. It was longer than I was, and about as thick as my wrist. Now in that book, ole Robin Hood had used a quarterstaff to fight a guy bigger than him, named Little John, over who was going to back off the foot log they met on as they went to cross a creek. A quarterstaff was what they used when they didn't really want to kill somebody, just knock their block off. Priests, for instance, like Friar Tuck, who was supposed to be a man of peace, would carry one like it was a walking stick, but really was a weapon. That Friar Tuck had beaned many a crook who tried to rob him of money he had collected for the church. Or, maybe they wanted the booze he had on him, I forget which. You'll have to read the book for yourself if you want to check out the story I'm telling here.

Anyway, the fight didn't turn out in Robin Hood's favor. Little John, who wasn't really little, hit a homer and knocked Robin Hood in the water. But Robin Hood tricked Little John somehow, and knocked him in the creek, too, and made Little John carry him on his back to the creek bank.

Well, I wanted to be Robin Hood so bad I went into intensive training. I would go around whaling the daylights out of trees, dead limbs, tin cans, stuff like that. I even ruined a few rows of Mr. Paul Lowrance's cornfield. I would whirl that

13

quarterstaff and bring it down on a ripe watermelon (in whose field I'm not saying) and splatter juice all over the place. I practiced swinging the bottom end up from the ground to break a bad guy's jaw, or punching for the breadbasket, and I got pretty good handling that hickory pole. Excuse me…quarterstaff.

Mostly, I had to practice my technique alone, but one day I got my younger brother Mick to spar with me. I had cut an extra pole when I made my quarterstaff, because I always knew someday I was going to have to try it out on an opponent. Mick was two years younger than me, and he liked the idea that he could maybe actually whip me for once in a fight, if he could use a stick as big as that, so he took me up on the idea. We squared up, and I dazzled him with some twirling and jumping around swinging at the air. He punched me in the belly with the end of his pole while I was putting on the demonstration. Okay, buddy, I decided, if you aren't interested in me showing you how to use this thing, we'll just get on with the serious fighting.

I moved in on him, tapping him on the leg. He raised his staff to brain me, but I easily parried his blow. Then we circled and swung and knocked out sticks together for a few minutes. Suddenly, I saw an opening, and cracked Mick on the knee pretty hard. He yelled and grabbed his leg. Tears came in his eyes, and I could see he was mad. He hopped around a couple of times, then out of nowhere, he brought that pole of his over and down with all his might, aiming to bust my head. I managed to duck a little, but the pole raked down the side of my head and near about tore my right ear off. Man, it hurt like the devil, and bled. Mick saw I was mad and fixing to do something bad to get even, and he threw down his pole and ran. I took after him, leaving my quarterstaff on the ground. I wanted to kill him with my hands.

Mick rounded the corner of the house with me right on his shirt tail, and he was looking for somewhere safe. Just ahead there was nothing but the pigpen, surrounded by a four-foot fence. Mick didn't hesitate. He sailed over that fence going lickety-split, me right behind him. I dived over that fence and tackled him around the waist in mid-air. We both landed in…well, I said this was a pigpen, right? Where ol' Popeye, our 500-pound pig we raised from a runt lived. Where he did other things, too, and then he wallered it all around into a mud lolly.

We hit that mud lolly on our faces and slid for a good piece in the goo. We sat up, faces covered, clothes splattered and ruined, and we looked at each other. No way to recognize who either of us was. All I could see was the whites of Mick's eyes. I suppose I looked the same to him. Suddenly, we started to laugh. We laughed until our sides hurt. We rolled around until ole Popeye came over to stand and just look at us with his head turned sideways. When we couldn't breathe anymore, we got up and helped each other over the fence, and slogged over to the well to clean off. We were no longer Robin Hood and Little John. Rolling around in a hog pen does something to a romantic fantasy. Once again, we were just brothers.

Tough Guy

Anybody knows that boys are tougher than girls. I first learned this astounding fact at the age of ten, and it went right to my head.

One hot summer afternoon I was hanging around my grandmother's house in hopes she might make a pan of biscuits. When it became apparent that there was not going to be any baking until suppertime, I had to find something to do. So, I decided to put my new knowledge to a test. I picked a fight with Carolyn Ruth.

My aunt Carolyn was the baby of Granny's family, and only a few years older than me. We grew up together, worked the fields together, and she was more like a big sister than an aunt. I liked Carolyn fine. She had never done anything to me. But I had to have someone to try it out on, and there stood

Carolyn – in a flour sack dress, humming a little tune, just asking for it.

I walked up to her and threw her a couple of insults. She completely ignored me. Angered to be taken lightly, I called her something unprintable. She laughed in my face. That was always one of Carolyn's biggest faults...she was too dang hard to get riled up. It was frustrating. I was beginning to get mad, even if Carolyn wasn't. Taking a running start, I dived headfirst at her, elbows flailing, bare feet churning the ground. She held me off with a hand in my face and laughed harder as I tried to hook a heel behind her ankle to take her down.

Now I know that boys are tougher than girls, and you know that boys are tougher than girls, but somewhere down the line someone had apparently neglected to slip the news to Carolyn. She acted like she was plumb ignorant of the fact.

Suddenly I found my left wrist and my left ankle both locked in a grip like iron. My other foot left the ground and that ignorant girl began to whirl me around and around like a helicopter. She was laughing like it was some kind of game. The ground, the sky, trees...everything began to blur and my eyes started to film over with a red haze. This thing was getting serious. I mean, for heaven's sake, why hadn't somebody got the information through to Carolyn?

All at once she let me go, and I zoomed through the air like a shot. I hit the ground hard, and by the time I quit bouncing through the dust I looked like I had been rolled in flour. I looked up through the settling dust to see Carolyn leaning against a tree, laughing so hard she could barely stand up. My head was spinning from all the whirling, so I decided to just lie quiet for a spell until the dizziness passed, and think on it some. Seemed like to me I was going to have to recheck some of the information the older boys had shared with me on this subject.

I decided to let Carolyn off that time. But I'm still looking for the guy who started all that stuff about boys being tougher than girls.

Old Tip and His Mechanical Mule

Thompsy Holder was not a rich man, but it made me feel richer for having known him. He was a small man, not over five feet six inches in height, and slight in build. His head was bald and shiny, with a scruffy little trim of gray hair around the edges. A three-day growth of gray whiskers on his chin never seemed to diminish or grow longer. With a twinkle in his beady little eyes and a gap-toothed grin on his rugged face, he went about his daily business with an easy, cheerful demeanor. He was affectionately known to his friends and neighbors as "Tip."

The Holders lived about a mile up the road from us, just across the line in Chester County. They lived in a ramshackle unpainted house on a plot of land where the Garland Road and the Needmore Road come together. Old Tip used to tell us that the Needmore Road, little more than a narrow rutted trail in those days, was so named because it "needed more gravel." Thompsy was married to a very likable florid faced woman named Ellen. When I knew them they had two sons living at home, Toby and J.T., and a daughter named Frances. I believe they had another son named Louis who lived away off somewhere, but I don't recall having ever met him. J.T. was about my age. He and I and my younger brother Mick hung around together a lot.

These folks were farmers, like almost everyone else in our part of the country during those times immediately after the Great Depression. I never thought to ask if they owned their own place or if they sharecropped. They obviously weren't rich, but they always had enough to eat – at least they did the times I ate with them. Some of the neighbors made a little moonshine from time to time to augment their income, but I don't know about old Tip. I do have it on good authority that he was known to take a sip of "shine" once in a while. My mother, who had known the family since her youth, told of a time when Tip was supposed to help her daddy do some work, and he didn't show up. They went looking and finally found him passed out in a springhouse, smelling like a brewery and grinning like a happy idiot.

Old Tip's wardrobe was simple...a faded pair of DC bib overalls (he pronounced it "overhauls") in the summertime, and that was it. He might occasionally wear a shirt, if he could find one, and if the day wasn't too hot and sticky. If he was going to have to – perish the thought – go out in the fields and work, he'd slap an old greasy cap on his head, to keep the sun from blistering his shiny dome. I suppose he must have had a pair of brogans to wear in the winter, or for one of his infrequent trips into town, but he didn't need them in the summer. What does a man need shoes for when he's got callous on his feet thicker than a shoe sole? I once saw him step right in the middle of a low-growing rose bush, thorns and all, and he didn't even flinch.

Plenty of fine clothes, big fine home, big fine car...

Ellen was always going on about finding Frances a "feller." She liked to read the movie star magazines and dream. She had given up on hitting the big time herself, but she dreamed of success for her daughter. Frances liked her mama's ideas all right, too. A fancy big city feller with a big important job, or one of them rich Hollywood movie stars would be just about right. How they would meet and fall in love with Frances was always the weak part of their plan. The corner of Needmore and Garland Bottom roads was a long way from the corner of Hollywood and Vine. Also, though Frances was nice enough looking, she wasn't exactly a look-alike for any of the movie queens of that day. But on certain important points Ellen and Frances would always agree: this "feller" had to be A: handsome, and B: rich, with a big, fine home and a big, fine car...and he would buy Frances plenty of fine clothes.

So they dreamed away, and it was fun listening to them. What difference did it make if Hollywood was two thousand miles away and all the rich and famous "fellers" already had more girls than they could handle on waiting lists? There was no need to confuse the issue with facts. A little harmless imagination mixed with a little naivety can make a dull, uneventful life seem awfully exciting.

21

After all, isn't anything and everything possible in America?

Baptizing in the river

One day I was up at J.T.'s house and we heard his mama talking about a baptizing some Holiness church people were having down in the Forked Deer River at the bridge in Garland Bottom. We had never been to a baptizing, and we were both pretty curious about how those holy rollers did it. Me and J.T. looked at each other. "Mama," J.T. said to Ellen, "Is it okay if me and Joe go down and sit on the bridge and watch the baptizing?"

Ellen considered it for a moment. "Yes, I suppose so," she said. "You can go on down there and set and watch. But now, J.T., if y'uns fall in that canal and get drownded, I'm gonna whup you when you get home!"

Walking down the road to the river we tried to think that one through, but we didn't get anywhere with it.

By the time we got to the place, the Holiness folks had already started. Some of them had climbed back up on the bank, shivering and wet, to dry off in the sun. There was a bunch of folks, men and women and young people, all wearing white robes. I had heard tell of the Holy Ghost, and that's what they made me think of – ghosts. I felt a chill go down my spine. In my mind I tried out a thought: These folks called themselves Holiness (or maybe it was others called them that)...maybe that's where the term "Holy Ghost" came from?

A few years passed before I began to read the Bible for myself and found out that the Holy Spirit is a person, and that person is God...and that a person who believes in Jesus can be filled with the Holy Spirit and have the power to live a Christian life.

But I didn't know any of that then. Me and J.T., two little barefoot boys, sat there swinging our feet off the edge of the old wooden bridge, watching wide-eyed as the minister ducked one after another under the muddy waters of the Forked Deer. As we watched the spectacle in wonder, I had no way of knowing that I myself would one day be baptized in water, and finally understand the meaning: symbolically entering into the death, burial and resurrection of Jesus Christ, my Lord. How little I understood then, and sometimes it seems I understand less now, but I go on learning. The images are still there, in the storehouse of memory, adding to my understanding of it all.

Reminds me of a preacher I heard about who liked to make sure people were baptized real good. He would hold folks under water a long time, while he prayed and made sure all the sin was washed away. One day he was baptizing a nervous looking old boy...got him dunked under the water and started to pray. Suddenly the guy commenced to jerking and thrashing around, trying to get away. The parson, a pretty husky old boy, just took a tighter grip and continued to pray, holding his man under by main strength. Bubbles floated up, and the preacher could hear something that sounded like words. The best he could make out, it sounded something like, "Oddey oddey oxin! Oddey oddey oxin!"

In due time the preacher said "Amen," and raised his poor victim out of the water, red-faced and bug-eyed. "Now what were you trying to say, son?" the preacher asked.

But the guy was already halfway to the river bank, splashing water wildly in every direction in his haste. The preacher caught his answer as he clawed his way up the bank:

"I said, *I seen a water moxican!*"

Sad day for a tractor salesman

The way it looked to me, Tip Holder was a horse trader by calling, if a calling is doing what a body enjoys and does best. Old Tip always seemed to have a few horses or mules about, and they changed from time to time. I remember a fine little black Morgan mare named Dixie that J.T. used to ride. There was a fat little pinto that they rode too. They also had a big, skinny pinto with a backbone like a razor blade. That was the horse I always ended up with when I went riding with J.T.

Old Tip had never plowed with anything other than a horse or a mule. That's how he liked it. He had no intentions of farming more than forty acres, and he could handle that much with a couple of mules, no problem. He understood mules and horses, and they understood him. He enjoyed fooling with them.

One fine summer day a big truck with a lowboy trailer behind slowed and pulled up on the side of the road in front of Thompsy's house. Tied down to the trailer sat a brand spanking new bright orange Allis Chalmers tractor. The driver's door opened on the truck and a well-fed citified dude in a tan field jacket and a grey felt country gentleman hat got out and strolled over to where old Tip sat on the ground, leaning back against a tree, resting in the shade. The dude tipped his hat, revealing thick brown hair, parted in the middle and plastered down. A wide, toothy grin split his square face.

"Mister Holder," he began, consulting a three-by-five index card he held in his hand, "I am a tractor salesman." He gave his name and reached to shake old Tip's hand. Tip wrinkled his nose at the smell of the guy's aftershave. "I have come all the way out here from Henderson to sell you this fine tractor," the man continued, with a theatrical sweep of his hat in the direction of the machine on the trailer.

Tip rolled his eyes sideways at the tractor, sitting there so shiny in the sun, looking like a Christmas ornament.

"No thankee, mister," he said. "She's purty as a picture, but I ain't got no use for a tractor. Got me a mule." He pulled his mumble-peg knife out of the ground and began gouging at the dirt under one horny toenail. Realizing that after finishing that toe he still had nine to go, he let out a defeated sigh and gave it up. He folded the knife and dropped it into a hip pocket.

But the salesman was not one to take no for an answer. He had a new Buick that wasn't paid for, and he needed to make a sale. He launched enthusiastically into a rehearsed spiel about how tractors don't eat corn like mules do, and how they could cover so much more ground in a day, etc. He rattled on and on until Tip was about ready to decide he was going to have to promise to buy the blamed thing just to get the dude to leave.

"Tell you what, Mister Holder," the salesman said, "I'll just unload her and you can take her for a trial run!" He was talking over his shoulder as he walked away, not giving Tip a chance to refuse. "Can't hurt to just drive it, you know."

The dude didn't know how wrong he was.

"Don't know how to drive no machinery," Tip objected, standing up. The mumble-peg knife fell through the hole in his back pocket. He scratched his head, inspecting the tractor more closely. "That thing ain't even got no plowlines to guide 'er with!"

Ignoring him, the salesman concentrated on backing the tractor off the trailer. He wheeled pop-pop-popping over to where Tip stood. "You just use this here steering wheel to guide her with," he said, jumping down from the seat. He patted a metal step. "Come on and climb up here, Mister Holder, and I'll show you how she works."

With a shrug, old Tip reluctantly climbed up and took a seat. The eager salesman ran through all the instructions, showed Tip how to work the gas, and then old Tip was off and rolling. He eased the big orange tractor out into last year's cotton patch and was going along pretty smooth and fairly straight. Confidence building, Tip reached over and pushed the gas lever all the way down. The popping got faster and louder, and the wind got cool in his face. Hot dang, old Tip was thinking, if this ain't fun!

Then he spied the fence at the end of the row.

Leaning back in the seat, Tip pulled back on the steering wheel. "Whoa!" he yelled. Nothing happened. That fence kept on coming at him pretty fast. The adrenaline rush lent strength to him as he braced his bare feet up against the dashboard and pulled back on the steering wheel with all his might. Eyes popping out of his head, veins bulging in his neck, ol' Tip went through four strands of barbed wire screaming, "Whoaback, you jughead, WHOA!"

Old Tip, tractor and fence disappeared over in the gulley in a cloud of red dust. Clanking and popping sounds, mixed in with a lot of cussing, wafted back to the stricken salesman, whose white knuckles clutched at the bark of a sturdy oak tree for support.

Presently the grimy, limping figure of old Tip emerged from the hanging cloud of dust, and stalked over to the gawking salesman. His overalls hung in rags from his skinny body, and his arms and face were crisscrossed with numerous scratches. "Eye-gonnies, mister," he snarled, "you git you and that ornery piece of junk offen my place." As short as he was, old Tip was looking pretty mean. "Anything that don't understand 'gee' and 'haw' and 'whoaback' just ain't no use to me!"

Later that afternoon neighbors along the road saw the truck and trailer go by, headed for town. They wondered who had traded in the dilapidated tractor that was piled on the trailer. That salesman must have needed a sale mighty bad to have taken a beatup old pile of junk like that in trade...all dusty and snarled in bobwire, with the steering wheel bent all doubled back toward the seat like that.

Just no accounting for them town salesmen.

Darts In A Salesman's Leg

My brother Mick was only about six or seven years old, and me a couple of years older the only time I ever saw him so totally stumped that he couldn't even think of some kind of wisecrack comeback.

The two of us were sitting on a homemade wooden bench down at the Five Points grocery store, our favorite hangout in the summer when school was out. We lived about a half mile from the store, on Hart's Bridge Road. We did our best to stay away from the house as much as possible because one of us, either me or Mick, or our older brother Jerry, would invariably forget ourselves at some point and, in our suffocating boredom, utter the thoughtless words, "There ain't nothing to do." You didn't say things like that around our mama unless you wanted to be put to work. She'd stick a broom, or a hoe, or a rake in your hand. It was a lot more fun to hang around the store and play a little baseball with Doc Lowrance, the storekeeper's son, or listen to the Exlax salesman explain the virtues of his product, or watch the severed head of a snapping turtle (whose body Doc's mama was cooking) bite a metal clothesline wire in two.

On this particular day, me and Mick were sitting there on the bench reading funny books. Paul Lowrance, the storekeeper, had gotten a whole rack of comics in, the ones that were left over when the new ones came out, and they would tear the corners off the covers and sell them at half price. Mr. Paul had them on the rack at a nickel apiece. Me and Mick had already read five or six each, trying to find one we liked enough to buy. We only had one nickel between us, so, we had to find one both of us liked enough to spend our nickel on.

A skinny salesman with a big nose and slicked-down hair came in and stood at the counter talking to Paul. Mick's attention wandered from his comic book to the salesman, who stood with his back to us. He was wearing a white shirt, plastered to his back by sweat, and black city pants with a shiny seat. Mick poked me with an elbow and, his face hidden behind his comic book, looked at me and flashed that wicked grin he had. He pointed at his shirt pocket. We were both dressed about alike in long legged khaki pants and short-sleeved shirts. Mick could never get his shirt buttoned straight, and the bottom always hung uneven. Most times I didn't even bother to button mine, except when Mama was around.

What Mick showed me, stuck in the loose part of his shirt pocket, was two darts he had made out of a couple of Mama's sewing needles and two matchsticks. To make the darts he had first struck the matches and put them out immediately, scrubbing the ash off the end. Then he shoved the eye part of the needle deep into one end and wrapped it securely with sewing thread, giving that end a little more weight. With his pocket knife he made a slit in the other end of the matchstick and inserted a little wedge of notebook paper, which he folded to give it an aerodynamic feather that made the dart fly straighter. Now Mick looked significantly at the salesman's rear end and back to me. Then he pointed at his darts again and winked, to make sure I got it.

He pulls out the first dart and aims. But then the guy shifts his weight and the seat of his pants goes slack. Now the fabric is stretched tight over the calf of his leg. Mick shrugs, readjusts his aim, squinting, with his mouth all twisted up, and lets fly. By the time the dart hits, Mick has his head buried innocently in the comic book again.

But the expected "Ow!" does not come. Mick looks at me and slowly peeps over the top of his funny book. The dart is sticking there, right where Mick aimed it, but the salesman is still calmly discussing the price of soda pop with the storekeeper. Mick pulls out his other dart. I can tell he's a little disturbed that his first missile didn't get the proper reaction. This time he chunks harder, and ducks behind his comic book again. He waits, but when the guy doesn't holler, Mick throws his comic book down. The second dart is sticking right there beside the other one, but the guy apparently isn't aware of it.

Mick grinds his teeth. He's never had this much trouble messing up someone's day before.

Mick jumps down off the bench, determined to keep his reputation intact. He tiptoes across the wooden floor on silent bare feet and crouches at the salesman's heels. He looks up to make sure the guy doesn't notice him. Then he grabs the salesman's pants at the cuff, yanks the fabric really tight against the calf of the man's leg, and pulls one of those darts out. He does all this in a millisecond, all in one motion, and starts stabbing the guy's leg with the dart as fast as his hand can move. *Jabbetyjabbetyjabbetyjab!* Then he jumps back out of the way before the salesman can get him with a kick.

The guy doesn't blink an eye. He just looks down when he notices there's a kid jumping around behind him, and when he sees the darts and realizes what's going on he busts out laughing. Paul, the storekeeper, looks over the counter to see what is happening, and he busts out laughing too. The two men are howling and wheezing, collapsed across the counter, slapping it with their hands. Mick is standing there, red in the face with frustration. He knew the needle-dart trick worked, and I did too, because he had tested it on me. Why the heck wasn't it working on that blasted salesman?

When the salesman had regained sufficient strength to push himself off the counter, he decided Mick deserved some kind of an explanation. Chuckling, he bent down and raised the leg of his pants to his knee. Mick's face went white and his mouth flew open. Of all th'…! *The guy had a wooden leg!*

The expression on Mick's face was priceless. Paul and the salesman howled with laughter again. It was humiliating. Mick turned without a word and with a beet-red face marched out of the store, his back stiff as a board. Dropping my comic books on the bench, I followed him, knowing I'd just seen something that few people had ever seen – my mischievous little brother, speechless. Mick didn't wait for me to catch up. When he got home he marched up on the front porch, in the front door and, without pausing to speak a word to anyone, went straight out the back door and into the woods. He stayed there, sitting on a stump, fuming until suppertime.

Mick wasn't fit to live with for a week after that. For once, the joke was on him.

Mulligan's Fancy Britches

On my best day I was never able to pick more than two hundred and fifty pounds of cotton. My average was more like a hundred, or one-fifty. I always tried to pick it too clean. And, I'll have to admit...I day-dreamed a lot. But I knew a lot of hands who could pick 300 pounds if they had the right incentive. Like if they were taking in a Gene Autry movie that night with a girl, and needed a little extra cash for a milk shake or something afterward. I guess I just never had that much incentive.

I once saw Wayne Williams and Jerry Lowrance in a boll-pulling contest. Pulling bolls is what you do after the cotton has been picked over two or three times and there's not much left to glean except a few scraps that were missed and whatever could be had from the half-opened bolls that probably would never have time to open fully because it was too late in the year. The quality of the cotton is not as good, but there was a little money in it. Every pound counts when you're a cotton farmer.

Wayne and Jerry got down on their knees in the dirt, each taking two rows of picked-over cotton. At a word, they threw themselves forward, nine-foot long canvas cotton sacks trailing behind them. If a person can run on their knees, they were doing it. Bits of cotton stalk, lint and other debris flew into the air as they forged ahead, elbows flying like windmills. Those boys must have weighed up three hundred pounds each that day. They had bolls, leaves, stalks, clods and bits of brick in those cotton sacks when they dumped the sacks in the wagon.

But there is only one man who stands out in my mind as the cotton-pickingest man I ever saw. His name was William Mulligan. The Mulligans lived across the woods from us, him and her and an uncounted number of kids. Some people might have considered them white trash, but not my Mama. White trash, she said, was people who were too sorry to work. The Mulligan's worked every day, and they worked hard. But they were uneducated, and the field work they did was never enough to feed all those kids and have any left over. So, they were never able to get ahead. Even so, they were happy. Mama went to their house one time and saw they didn't have anything to eat off of. She gave them a set of dishes out of her own kitchen. The next time Mama went over to check on them, every single one of those dishes had been broken by that bunch of wild kids, and they were eating off lard can lids. This really happened.

It took a lot to feed a family like that, and Mulligan was kept busy providing. His wife worked in the fields too, and she could actually pick more cotton than her husband. Mulligan was a big muscle-bound man with big ears sticking out from the close-cropped sides of his head. His wife had done some home barbering by turning a bowl over his head and cutting everything that grew beneath the rim. A thick stand of black hair clumped on top, giving his head the look of a floor mop. Not sophisticated, but it was cheap.

Mulligan could pick 400 pounds of cotton a day without breaking a sweat. You may think I'm lying, but that's the gospel truth. At a nickel a pound, the going price for the times, they didn't do too bad, both of them working.

Mrs. Mulligan was not a delicate woman herself. She stood about as tall as her husband, and talked twice as rough. She consistently picked more cotton than him. Anyone who hired both of them could count on getting his cotton to the gin ahead of the other wagons. My uncle Jim hired Mrs. Mulligan once to help him pick out a small field on a slope near Granny's house. All her kids but one were either out working somewhere else, or being taken care of by one of the older girls at home. The youngest was still in diapers, but was old enough to walk. I was helping Jim that day, too, and I couldn't tell if the kid was a boy or a girl. She had him (or her?) sitting on a pallet under the shade of the wagon, tethered to one of the wheel spokes by a long, twisted strip of sheet, like a homemade rope. The baby must have gotten thirsty or something because it started squalling. Mrs. Mulligan paid it no mind, just kept on stuffing her cotton sack with cotton. Jim, he kept eying the baby somewhat apprehensively. He saw that the poor child was getting tangled in the chord and was tugging mightily to pull free. Suddenly Jim let out a yell, threw his cotton sack strap off his shoulder and took off running. I looked up and saw the problem.

The Mulligan kid, it seemed, had inherited some of the family strength. The wagon was parked at a slant on the hillside with the tongue dragging the ground. Believe it or not, that kid had tugged and squalled and pulled so hard trying to get to its mama that the wagon wheel had actually begun to move. In another second the wagon would be rolling down the hill. Jim made it to the wagon just in time and began undoing the rope around the kid's waist. He'd been feeling sorry for the little tyke anyway, all tied up like that. Jim had been a prisoner of war in Germany once, and he knew what it was like to have your freedom taken away.

Mrs. Mulligan exploded. "You leave that baby alone!" she snapped at Jim, and began loosening herself from her cotton sack. Mrs. Mulligan, as I said, was about the same size as her husband, big boned and hard faced. She had on several layers of patched clothing, including a couple of shirts put on over a flower sack dress, and wore pants underneath the dress. A straw hat tied down with a scarf hid her sweaty face, but Jim could still see it was red as she came up the hill at him. He backed off in a hurry, and his own face turned red as Mrs. Mulligan gave him a good dressing down for messing with her kid. She got the child straightened out and gave it some water while Jim went muttering back to his work. Try to help somebody and they give you a flogging. Jim wasn't much of a hand to advise people on how to handle their kids after that.

William Mulligan never tried to make his way by his wits. I reckon he was so stout he didn't need wits. All he knew was to bow his neck and grab hold, and anything he laid his hand to was going to move, one way or another. I heard my uncle Ben tell about one time when Mulligan was working at the sawmill and one end of a huge log rolled off the carriage. The other workers rushed over to help lift the log back into place. But before they could lay hands on it, Mulligan had put his shoulder under it, put it back in place on the carriage, and was dusting off his hands. Ben said when Mulligan lifted that log his arms split the sleeves out of his shirt.

Mulligan was bull strong all right, but he was no dummy. He talked like he had reasonably good sense. But he had come up hard and poor, and all he'd ever known was to work. Probably he had never in his life given thought to making a living in any other way except by the sweat of his brow. I never heard of his family being on welfare, though folks like my mother would give them stuff from time to time. Some folks thought him ignorant, and he did some things that caused folks to laugh at him. But ignorance can't always be helped when a person has no opportunity to get any schooling. Me, I believe this country needs more men like Mulligan. When you paid him for a day's work you got something for your money. Of course, we need planners too, but when the big plans are all laid out, and everything is all organized and decided on, there still has to be someone to put his back under the load and lift. This country was built by the Mulligans just as much as by the big industrialists and financiers. I have a lot of respect for who Mulligan was, and what he was. I wouldn't make fun of him one bit. Certainly not to his face.

However, it was hard to keep from laughing at some of the things Mulligan did. He and his family were always so proud of anything people gave them. Some things they didn't know how to take care of, like the dishes, because they'd never really been taught.

I remember once Mama took them a big box full of clothes, stuff we'd outgrown but was still serviceable. You'd have thought Santa Claus had come. They had such a happy time laying everything out and matching up each item to who it fit. Mama said she got more of a blessing than they did. Just watching the way their faces would light up when one of them would pull something pretty out of the box, and watching how they took on over it, was all the payment Mama needed. Most of the stuff was old, but it might as well have just come off the rack at J.C. Penney's, the way they carried on. There was a nice pair of satiny black ladies' slacks that Mama had thrown in because after she bought them she found they were too big for her. She thought that Mrs. Mulligan might like them, as they were a little more dressy than the usual attire she wore to the field.

My uncle Pete came in laughing one Saturday afternoon, and told us a story. He and Mulligan had gone into Jackson together that morning to see the sights, take care of some business, and maybe play a little pool. Mulligan was all slicked up, looking pretty nice. He'd plastered his cowlick down with lard, and he'd shaved. His brogans were shined, and he had on a clean shirt. Something about the black pants he had on looked out of place, but Pete couldn't decide what it was. The pants were a bit tight, but then everything fit Mulligan tight. The legs were too short...maybe that was it. Or maybe the shine of the material.

The two of them went into Joe's Poolroom and shot a few games. They drank a few cold bottles of brew, and eventually the beer began to have its effect. Before long Mulligan announced, "Pete, I gotta go see a man about a dog."

Having drunk about the same number of beers as Mulligan, Pete had coincidentally developed an interest in the same dog, so they both racked their cue sticks and headed for the john.

They walked into the men's room and squared off. That's when Pete finally figured out what it was that had been bothering him about Mulligan's new pants.

He happened to glance over and there was Mulligan, struggling and groping to reach around and unzip those women's pants from behind!

Hammerhead's Big Indian

Hammerhead Rouse walked into Paul Lowrance's Five Points Grocery one day, and he was limping on the side that had the wooden leg. His face was red, and he was muttering to himself.

"What's the matter, Hammerhead?" Paul asked. "Your tobakker not agreeing with you, or something?"

Hammerhead snorted. He leaned his wiry frame against the counter and wiped a mop of sandy colored hair out of his sweaty face. "Aw, it's that dang big ol' Indian motorsickle of mine," he fumed. "I oughtta bust that thing in a million pieces and sink it in a swamp!"

He continued to mumble irritably under his breath while reaching deep into the cold drink box for an ice-cold RC Cola. Paul waited silently with a raised eyebrow. He cut off a slice of hoop cheese, put it on a square of waxed paper and slid it across the counter in front of Hammerhead. He figured if an explanation was forthcoming the man would get around to it without any prompting. Paul wasn't much for prying into another man's business. He had never even inquired about how Hammerhead got such an unusual name. No doubt it had something to do with the thickness of his skull.

Hammerhead opened the RC, turned it up and killed about half of it before slamming the bottle on the counter with a satisfied sigh. He wiped a grimy hand across his mouth and bit off a hunk of the hoop cheese, explaining as he chewed:

"I was headin' outta Jackson on the Hart's Bridge Road, not doin' much over seventy or eighty. I was havin' to lay that old Indian down pretty low in some of them curves comin' through Liberty Grove, and that's when I commenced to smellin' smoke. Well, I glanced around to see if they was burnin' off a field, or a dozer pile or sump'n.' But I didn't see nothin'." Hammerhead paused to take another bite of cheese and washed it down with the rest of the RC.

"Comin' across the Forked Deer bottom I quit smellin' smoke, so I didn't give it no more thought. Then I come to Mason Wells and had to lean 'way over in that steep curve in front of Iry Allen's...then I noticed the smoke again. I figgered maybe I better stop and see if there was something wrong with my machine." Hammerhead finished the cheese and wiped his hands on the front of his shirt. Suspecting the end of the story would be worth the wait, Paul leaned his elbows on the counter, patiently giving Hammerhead time to get his breath.

"So, I pulled over to the side, put the kickstand down and got off...and blamed near fell in the sand ditch! Then I seen where the smoke was comin' from."

"What was it?" Paul asked, unable to contain his curiosity any longer. "A blown oil seal or a hole in your muffler?"

"Naw, naw, nothin' like that," Hammerhead said impatiently. "You know I nacherly ain't got no feelin' in my wooden leg?"

Paul nodded. "Nacherly."

"Well, see, that's what happened. I never noticed that my foot on that side had done slipped off the foot rest. So, every time I leaned into a curve on that side, that dang foot would get caught under the pedal and scrape the ground."

He held up the foot in question, turning it to reveal a blackened stump sticking through a ragged shoe with no sole. Paul was gripping the counter, trying to hold back his laughter. He didn't believe it was right to laugh at a body's handicap. But he lost the battle, and the counter began to shake.

Hammerhead noticed the RC bottle skittering around on the counter top and looked up. His face got red. "Go ahead and laugh, dagnabbit!" he snapped. "It ain't the shoe I mind so much...the shoe shop can fix that. But who in the heck am I gonna get to resole my *foot?*"

Mule School

Old Bill

"Lord how mercy! He's killin' the mule!" Granny wailed, launching her arthritic body out the back door as if she were twenty again. She went streaking toward the barn, dishrag waving in the air.

Me and my little brother Mick went to the enclosed back porch and took a look out the screen door to see what the commotion was all about. From the direction of the barn we heard someone swearing profanely, and an animal squealing in fright. We went goggle-eyed when we saw our uncle Pete was beating Old Bill, his big black plow mule, with a flat steel car spring. It was not a sight for young eyes to see. So, naturally me and Mick had to see it. We jumped off the back steps and left little puffs of dust behind us as we loped along the path to the barn behind Granny.

Pete was poison mad. His face was so red it was almost purple. He had hitched Old Bill to a tree with a stout rope, and was seriously engaged in thrashing the stubbornness out of that mule. Poor Old Bill must have gee'd once too often when he was supposed to haw, or something. He'd finally snapped the pucker string on Pete's patience. He wanted to dance, so Pete was going to make him pay the fiddler.

Granny saw she wasn't going to be able to do anything with Pete. His eyes had already glazed over with a murderous red film. He was in a world where earthling voices couldn't contact him. Finally, Granny quit trying to plead with him and turned hopelessly away. Covering her ears to shut out the profanity and pain, she limped slowly back to the house, muttering fearsome predictions under her breath.

Me and Mick, we ducked around behind Old Bill's flying hooves and went up the hall gate into the barn loft where we could see better. Up there we had us a ringside seat. We didn't want to stop Pete. We thought it would be fun to watch a man beat his mule to death with a car spring.

Spellbound, we watched, gripping the rough floor boards of the barn loft, our bare feet hanging over the edge. Safely out of the way, we surrendered ourselves to the spectacle, totally fascinated by the kicking, plunging, cussing, dusty tableau below. Ol' Pete was sure giving himself a good workout, if he didn't bust a vein.

He would draw back, holding that car spring in both hands like a baseball bat, and swing on that mule's broad side with all his might – Boom! Right in the ribs. BOOM! BOOM! BOOM!

Old Bill would jump and kick and squall with every lick, and try to lunge away to the other side of the tree. I thought surely he would break the rope or his bridle any minute, but the rope held snug. Pete kept thumping his dusty hide until the poor mule wound the rope so tight around the tree that it pulled his nose up against the bark. Nostrils flaring, snorting with fear, eyes rolled back until the whites showed, Old Bill stood trembling while Pete walked around on the other side and drew back to bat left handed. Then the fun started all over again.

By the time he had wound that old mule back around the tree, Pete had just about exhausted himself, physically, emotionally, and linguistically. With a final horrible oath, he slung the car spring away and began to unloose the mule from the tree. Pete's shirt tail was hanging out, and he was wringing wet. His sweaty hair strung down in his face, plastered to his skin. He was trembling as bad as the mule. But when he looked up and saw me and Mick hanging on to the edge of the barn loft, we could see that there was somebody home behind the eyes once more.

It's common knowledge that mules can't think, of course. But Pete led an extremely *alert* plowmule away from the whuppin' tree that day, and I could almost see the wheels turning between Old Bill's fuzzy black ears. In his mind I know he had his slide rule out, planning with scientific accuracy just how precisely straight each and every one of the remaining furrows in that field would be, should the mule god only see fit to allow him to step into those traces one more time.

Any mule that worked for my uncle Pete soon learned that he would get no sympathy trying to pull the old, time-honored stubborn mule act. Stubbornness, he found, was not exclusive to muledom.

Old Jake

I never saw Pete get that mad at a mule again, except once. Actually, by the time I arrived at the scene to see the fun, Pete wasn't even mad anymore. He was just standing there in the field with a smoking shotgun dangling from his hand, shaking his head wearily. At his feet, in a heap beside the overturned plow in the freshly turned soil, lay Old Jake, the buckskin mule who was twice as old as Pete, and perhaps twice as stubborn. Old Jake had a bloody hole as big as my fist in his side. He was breathing fast and hard, in shock. I figured he was getting ready to die.

Old Jake was a jumper. He could stand flat-footed and jump a four-strand barbwire fence. Then Pete would have to go through the routine of rounding the mule up and putting him back in the pasture. By the time Pete got back to the barn to hang up the bridle that dang mule would be calmly grazing outside the fence again. It was maddening.

Pete wasn't exactly the type person a body could point to as an example of patience. Pete's daddy died when Pete was fourteen, right at the beginning of World War Two. All of Pete's older brothers were off in the Army and Navy, and Pete had to quit school to run the farm. It must have scared him to think of all the responsibility that was his, a fourteen-year-old kid having to be the man of the family.

Pete did what he had to do, and he did it well. He and his younger brother Wayne and their sisters at home kept things going until the war was over and their oldest brother Jim returned to take over. But the weight of responsibility on a skinny kid who would rather have had his daddy alive again, and himself chasing giggling girls at school, left little room in Pete Williams for patience. He didn't have the luxury. Just the worry of how to get it all done was enough, without the additional frustration of having to spend all day rounding up a fence-jumping mule before you could begin a day's work.

Understandably, Pete's fuse was a mite short in those days. So, it's no wonder Granny saw fire in his eyes that day when he came stalking into the house looking like he wanted to kill something. He went into his bedroom and came out loading the shotgun. He left the house and started down toward the field behind the pear orchard. Granny jumped up and grabbed her shoes and bonnet, but before she could get out of the house to stop him, she heard a loud BOOM! from down behind the garden fence. Heart in her throat, Granny hurried as fast as she could go through the tall weeds to see what had happened, afraid of what she would find. I swan, three boys in the war were scarcely more worry than that high-tempered young-un down there in the field with the shotgun!

This time it was my older brother Jerry and me who heard the rookus and came fogging over the hill from our house. Not that the sound of a shotgun going off in hunting country was remarkable - except when accompanied by the braying of a terrified mule, followed by the hysterical screams of a woman.

So, there we are – Granny, Jerry and me, standing in a semicircle, and Pete in the middle holding a smoking shotgun in his hand, shaking his head sadly. And Old Jake lying on the ground with a gaping hole in his heaving side, goggle-eyed and scared. We thought at first that Pete had finally popped his cork.

Pete started to lift the shotgun, and I thought, oh, no – he's sorry for what he's done, and now he's fixin' to put a round through his own head! But Pete only ejected the spent hull and slung the empty shotgun over his shoulder. He turned and looked at Jerry and me. He had the saddest look on his face that I have ever seen.

"You boys see now what a temper can do for you," he said, and turned and walked away.

Old Jake didn't die. I guess Pete went to get some tweezers and salve, or something, and fixed him up. The wound wasn't really all that serious anyway. You can't kill a mule with a shotgun. You have to wait until they decide to die, just like you have to wait for them to decide when they're ready to do anything else.

The old buckskin was still jumping fences when he was forty, but I reckon Pete never used a shotgun on him again. Shotgun shells were cheap. Plow mules were not.

A Summer of Living Dangerously

Delivery Boy

I turned fourteen the summer I delivered groceries for my uncle Whit Griffin who owned a neighborhood grocery store on Lenoir Street in Jackson, Tennessee. Uncle Whit was married to my mother's sister, Betty Grace. This was in the days when neighborhood stores offered free delivery service to their regular customers.

When I worked there the delivery vehicle was a red Schwinn bicycle with a huge wire basket over the half-size front wheel. The Schwinn was a one-speed, not geared for climbing hills, or switching over for easy pedaling. When that gigantic basket was filled with groceries it took some kind of huffing and puffing just to get the whole load moving. I built up some knotty legs that summer.

Nobody in that neighborhood of East Jackson had more than one car. Most didn't have any, and the ones who did had them for the husband to drive to work. Housewives were left to run the households without transportation. When those ladies bought groceries, they needed them delivered to their door. It wasn't a luxury – it was a necessity.

Delivery boys from the different stores were always crossing paths. The kid who delivered prescriptions for Hays Avenue Pharmacy was the envy of all. He sizzed around town on one of those small entry level Harley Davidsons they used to make. He never even worked up a sweat, the little punk. I'd see him zoom by trailing a plume of blue smoke and I'd itch to jerk him off that noisy wheel and bust him right in his weasel rat face. Me pumping my guts out in the hot sun, and him sitting up there in the middle of that padded seat not breaking a sweat. Just didn't seem fair.

One day I had to make a delivery to a section of the neighborhood that always smelled of chitlins. It was down on First Street in the low swampy ground along the creek.

There was an order from Miz Stitz, and another for two unmarried twin ladies who lived together in a shotgun shack on First. There was another small order somewhere in the neighborhood. I had a case of bottled Cokes in the bottom of the basket, with a watermelon on top. The groceries, including a dozen eggs, canned stuff, vegetables and meat, were sacked up and put in boxes, one to each customer.

The oversized basket was overloaded when I pushed the bike off its sturdy kickstand. Luckily, First Street was on a slope that fell away behind the store, making it easier for me to get the load underway without too much wobbling. After crossing Belmont, I didn't even have to pedal. Actually, it was necessary to keep light pressure on the brakes to keep from building up too much speed as I coasted down the increasingly steep hill.

My first stop was at the twins' house. The strange thing about them was, they were white ladies. I thought it unusual for them to be living in an all-black neighborhood. I mentioned it to Raymond Trollinger one day. He was about my age, and hung around the store most all the time. He laughed and called me a dumb hillbilly.

"Them ladies is *albinos*, he said.

"What's a albino?" I asked.

"It means they ain't really white folk. They's black."

"Wait a minute…they're really black – but they're… *white?*"

It took a while for me to wrap my mind around that concept, but I figured old Raymond knew his neighborhood, so I took his word for it.

I put the bike up on its stand in front of the twins' house, a basic shotgun design, three rooms in a line…living room, bedroom and kitchen all the way in back. I lifted a box of groceries out of the basket, climbed the steps and stood on the narrow front porch, knocking on the much-painted and flaking door. From an open window smells were emerging that I identified as some kind of cooking, but whatever it was, it wasn't something that I ever wanted to eat. I moved to the other side of the door, away from the window, and knocked again.

"Come on in, honey!" someone bawled from the back of the house. "We back here in the kitchen whuppin' up a mess of chitlins."

I blinked. Growing up in the country, I knew what chitlins were. I'd heard about all the methods of cleaning them; creek-slung, stump-whupped, or blowed. But even if I could convince myself that the sanitizing process made pig guts fit'n' to eat, I could never get past the smell. Getting sprayed by a skunk right in the face, eyes wide open, would be like Chanel No. 5 by comparison. The deadly aroma of a snapping turtle twitching in a pot of boiling water is the only thing I can compare it to.

I waited until a puff of wind cleared the air momentarily, took in a mighty breath and held it as I opened the door. I hurried through the living room, giving a tight nod to the lady who had started for the front door to see who it was. Hurrying past her, I shot her another glance. She sure looked like a white lady to me.

"Go on back and set the groc'ries on the counter, honey," she told me. I nodded again, wide-eyed, and pushed on through the bedroom to the kitchen. I nudged the door open with my toe and braved it. Even holding my breath, I could feel the toxicity of the air. Blue steam rose from a bubbling pot on the stove. Flies, foolish enough to investigate the strange aroma, lay scattered around the counter and floor.

Usually I take the time to unpack the groceries and save the box for the next delivery, but I knew I'd never survive if I tried that this time. My face was already beginning to turn blue.

I couldn't hold my breath much longer. I dumped the groceries, box and all on the counter and beat it out the same way I came in. As I breezed through the living room I spoke to the lady there (boy, she really was *white!*). "You can keep the box ma-am," I said in a strained voice, letting out what little wind I had left. I was out the door, off the porch and into healthy air before I took a chance and sucked in a deep, satisfying breath again.

Showing Off Never Worked For Me

The next stop I made was up the hill on the other side of the ditch. I left some groceries at an address I can't remember, turned around and headed back down the hill. The last box of stuff, including watermelon, cokes and eggs, was tagged for the Stitz home.

As I started down the hill I saw two girls coming my way on their bikes. My heart jumped a little, because one of the girls was Linda Burleson, who I considered to be the prettiest girl in the neighborhood. She lived on Belmont, just a block behind the store. I had about two-thirds of a crush on her, but her daddy was a cop. I was always a little nervous about whether to let on about that other one-third.

Hey, maybe this was my opportunity to impress her a little. What if I got up some speed and went barreling down the hill like a maniac and blasted right through between the two girls? That oughtta get their attention.

So, genius that I am, I did that. Pumping furiously, I bore down upon them like a dive bomber. Their eyes widened as I got closer. Linda's black pony tail twitched back and forth as she looked nervously from side to side for a ditch to take. The other girl had red hair and eyes as big as saucers. Her name was Brenda Arnold. Just before we collided they hunched their shoulders, closed their eyes and screamed in harmony at the top of their voices. I was Rocket Man, a tornado, a hurricane as I roared past right between them, almost blowing them off their bikes.

It was delicious. I had goose bumps going up and down my back. Did you see the expression on their faces? Sitting straight and proud in the saddle, I was laughing deliriously as I began to lean into the turn onto the street where Miz Stitz lived. A little late I realized that I might have built up a mite too much velocity to be able to comfortably negotiate the ninety-degree turn without going off the pavement into the dirt.   The   dirt in the corner wasn't dirt. It was sand. *Loose* sand.

I hit that loose sand with my shirt tail popping straight out behind me, and buried that little bitty front wheel up to the axle. The effect was immediate and dramatic. The front wheel went no farther, while the rest of the bicycle continued on, as did I... and as did Miz Stitz's groceries. The back end of the bike whipped around and snapped me over the basket like a hundred-pound sack of chicken feed. I landed on my back, sending up a mushroom of dust.

It never works for you, the voice inside my head told me, yet you always go into it believing you can pull it off. But it never works...it never works.

The dust settled, my head cleared, and I picked myself up, slapping at my clothes. I threw a sheepish look in the directions of the astonished girls. They were looking at me like, who was *that? What* was that?

They watched me slop around through the chunks of smashed watermelon picking up scattered bottles of Coke. They watched in fascination as one by one the bottles began to explode in my hand from the terrific heat and the shaking up. I averted my eyes in order to avoid seeing them fall off their bikes laughing.

I worked off my shame and frustration pedaling back up that steep hill to the store. In the July heat I began to forget my embarrassment and started to worry about heat stroke. I wondered if I would ever learn. I should have known better than to try to show off for a girl. It never works out like it's supposed to.

But it did get their attention.

And at least the eggs, amazingly, didn't break.

Miz Stitz and Sonny Dear

Back at the store I explained about the accident (leaving out minor details concerning girls) and went into the walk-in meat locker to sulk and cool off while Uncle Whit refilled Miz Stitz's order. Five minutes later I walked out of the cooler refreshed and good to go, the sweat on my body having turned into a fine film of frost. I got the Stitz order arranged in the basket and headed back down the hill. I didn't look at any girls this time. I figured Miz Stitz was beginning to wonder where her groceries were, so I wasted no time. I worried that Uncle Whit might dock my pay for the spoiled groceries, but he never had before. I only made thirteen dollars a week anyway.

Miz Stitz was not cooking chitlins when I knocked, thank goodness. She let me in and smiled when she saw the fat green watermelon. She was not a tiny woman herself. Let me put it this way…if you were the mailman and she came out to mail a letter, while she was standing there you would not be able to see her house.

The living room was not arranged in any logical order, or in any order at all. Stuff was scattered everywhere. There was a baby bed in one corner, the kind with bars, where one side slides up and down. Lying there in the bed was a kid. I thought it was a baby at first, until Miz Stitz shook the bed and said, "Wake up, Sonny dear. Tell Mama what you wants for breffus."

Breakfast? It was already past noon.

The kid rolled over, yawned and stretched. I asked how old the baby was, and she said, "Six."

Six? That was the tiniest six-year-old kid I ever saw. He sure didn't take after his mama. He was so skinny I could count his ribs when he stretched. He was dressed in nothing but an oversized pair of khaki shorts that came down to his ankles. He sat up and rubbed his eyes, in no hurry to be awake.

"Well, tell me, honey," Miz Stitz repeated. "What you wants for breffus?"

"Beer," Sonny said lazily, and lay back down.

I waited for the rebuke. There was none. I took the groceries on back to the kitchen to unload and left. As I went out the front door I heard the refrigerator door close in the kitchen.

None of my business, I said to myself as I rode away on my bike. *None of my business.*

Scary Movie

One of the boys who lived in the neighborhood was Robert Daly. He and I hung out together a lot. I heard he later became Chief of Police in Jackson, which is surprising, considering the rough crowd he used to associate with. Anyway, he was fun to be with. We got into some interesting things together.

One night we decided to go downtown to see a movie. We had to walk a mile or more down East Chester and over to Baltimore, where the two major theaters of Jackson stood side by side in all their brilliant splendor...the Paramount and the Malco. We couldn't wait to get inside.

We walked up to the entrance and looked up to see what was playing. There on the marquee, in two-foot high letters was one word..."FRANKENSTEIN." I felt chills go up and down my spine. That movie was without a doubt the scariest movie of all time. Made in 1931, it resurfaced periodically. This was the first time I had seen it.

I kept telling myself throughout the picture that the guy in the hairy suit with a railroad spike through his neck was just an actor. He wasn't really a monster. Creatures like that don't really exist. *Do they?*

Knowing it was really Boris Karloff, who was just an actor doing his job, didn't help much either. To us the name Boris Karloff inspired fully as much fear as did the name Frankenstein.

As the movie progressed toward the final hair-raising scene, Robert and I scrunched lower and lower in our seats, desperately cramming popcorn in our mouths, as if that would protect us – sort of like holding up a cross. Nobody ever got mangled by a berserk monster while eating popcorn.

When the movie was over we started home, surrounded by an aura of fear. Of course, neither of us would let on. We covered our anxiety by laughing and joking about what we would do to Boris Karloff if he came after us in his chunky steel boots. But something...*something* had changed about the neighborhood. It was getting late, and all those comfortable looking clapboard houses we had passed on the way to the picture show, windows ablaze with good cheer, had suddenly taken on an atmosphere of menace. The windows were now dark, like the hollow eyes of a skull. The houses were black, hulking shapes against the night sky. The shadows between them seemed to reach out to grab us as we passed. We hurried from the dim glow of one street light to another, imagining the gloomy areas of sidewalk to be peopled with unspeakable things that would snatch at our ankles. We were afraid to run, knowing something would grab us from behind if we did. The wind moaned. A cloud passed over the moon. It was a long way home.

Only a sense of humor sustained us. Robert Daly was a joker. He got ahead of me and hid behind a tree. I saw him do it. But I still screamed like a girl when he jumped out right in front of me and yelled, "Boo!"

He laughed until he was too weak to laugh any more. I recovered control of my bodily functions, and after that we felt a little better. We got a little of our confidence back, and continued on for a block or two, thinking we had shaken our fear. But I was waiting for a chance to get even. I spotted a place where some concrete steps came down to the sidewalk through a wall built up to protect the yard. I ran ahead and hid behind the corner of the wall. When Robert came even with me I leaped out of the shadows and yelled, "Boo!"

Nothing original, and it wasn't as if he didn't expect it, having watched me hide. But it worked like a charm anyway. He screamed and jumped like he'd stepped on a snake. I laughed myself sick, and by that time he was laughing too. It seemed ridiculously funny to us that we had come out of that movie so saturated with fear that even when we expected it and saw it coming we were still able to scare the life out of each other.

So, naturally, we kept doing it, all the way home. *Frankenstein* was one spooky movie, all right, but the trip home on the dark streets of East Jackson was five times as scary.

Unfriendly Territory

Robert Daly got us into another fine mess one night when he talked me into going with him down into the projects. Parkview Courts was a new development just across East Chester from the Parkview Baptist Church. The apartments were all alike, row upon row of red brick low-income housing, strung out in a rambling circle. As such government developments invariably do, the place soon became a slum. The night we went down there some of the apartments had not yet been occupied. But already the project was getting a reputation. It wasn't known as a good place to take a lot of moonlight strolls.

It turned out that's why Robert wanted me along. He was afraid to go down there alone. As he laid it out for me, there was someone who lived in Parkview Courts he wanted to pick a fight with, and he needed me to watch his back.

Among the rougher element who had moved into the projects there was some punk who had challenged Robert's manhood or something, and he wanted a chance to take this punk down. I would just be there for insurance. By the time it was over I was wishing I *had* insurance.

Of course, being a greenhorn in East Jackson, I had no hint of what it meant for a stranger to go boldly into Parkview Courts at night. As we entered the property we saw a dark figure standing alone on a grassy slope highlighted by the green glow of one of the few unbroken street lights in the project. Something about the figure didn't look right. The leather jacket fit the scene, but...maybe it was the jeans. A little too tight? *Something....*

Robert lifted a hand in greeting. The figure responded with a casual flip of the hand. I thought at first the hand was missing some fingers. It takes me a little time to figure some things out. Then the figure began smacking one fist into the opposite palm, slowly, emphatically...menacingly.

Then I saw the ponytail.

I hit the brakes. "This 'punk' is a *girl?*" I asked Robert. "You brought me down here to face off with a *girl?*"

"Don't jump to conclusions," he said with a tight face. We stopped before the girl and said hi. She was about our age, shorter than us, with a good figure, dressed in tight jeans and a leather jacket. She was trying to look as much like a boy as possible, and wasn't succeeding by a long shot. But she had the attitude.

Robert obviously knew her, and must have introduced me, but I don't remember her name. All I know is that she had what it took to back up the attitude. It gradually dawned on me that what my buddy really wanted was to be sweet on the girl, but she kept making him mad. As we talked, sitting in a circle on the grass, swatting at mosquitoes, the girl seemed to want to take offense to everything Robert said. As pretty as she was, his pride wouldn't allow him to overlook the sharpness of her tongue, and it wasn't long before he decided that by golly it was time to teach this irreverent female a lesson. He'd been getting madder and madder every time she challenged something he said. Finally, she made some crack that was the last straw, and he up and tied into her.

He rushed the girl, surprising her, and took her down on the ground. For a few minutes, I just sat there astonished, watching the two of them threshing back and forth on the turf. First one was on top, then the other. I could hardly tell them apart. Arms swinging, legs kicking, they struggled mightily, grunting and cursing. Then, out of the tangle of knees and elbows, I saw the girl sit upright. She was astraddle Daly and had him pinned to the ground with her knees on his arms. She was punching him in the face, and they weren't love taps.

"Joe...dang it!" Robert yelled, "Feel free to pitch in anytime!"

Without thinking, I dove at her and knocked her off Robert. Then a bee stung me on the nose. Then it stung me on the chin, then something hard as a brick hit me upside the head, and we were rolling over and over across the grass. She was beating the stuffings out of me. I don't know if I ever got in a good lick, but I got knees to the belly, an elbow to the jaw, head slammed into the ground, a punch to the goozle, and ended up in the same position Robert had ended up in – pinned to the ground, with that blasted punk female pounding me into jelly with her fists.

I would like to say that the two of us big, strong boys finally prevailed and taught that smart-alec girl a lesson she would not forget...but we didn't. The fight ended when she finally got tired of swinging and just quit.

Suddenly, strangely – everything smoothed out, and we were just three dirty, sweaty teenagers, lying in a circle on the grass, face up to the street light, wiping bloody noses, nursing split lips and talking calmly like nothing ever happened. Robert and the girl were getting on. I felt left out, but I sure as heck wasn't ready to get cross with *nobody* again right away. Actually, it felt kind of peaceful to just sort of lie there on the soft grass and talk quietly, with no stress in the air. With friends I had just... shared a moment with.

I don't know if Robert and the girl ever became an item. If so, he was welcome to her. One thing I was sure of...I never wanted to have a girlfriend I had to whip every time I went to see her.

The neighborhood. Nothing like it. Griffin's Grocery and the mean streets around it in East Jackson. Where else could you find a place where black people are white, acrobatic shows are free, where terror walks the streets and even the girls are men...and where else could a six-year-old get a beer for breakfast?

Child Raising Guerilla Style

I might not ought to tell this, because it throws me in a bad light. But, knowing there might be some poor, desperate parent or big brother out there somewhere who has come to the end of the rope, I'll go ahead. Maybe it will bring hope to the person who has the responsibility of taking care of a kid who will not follow instructions, no matter what you do to amuse them, promise to give them, or let them get away with. If it helps one person to maintain their sanity, it will be worth whatever criticism I might get.

Here's the situation: My dad and stepmother both had jobs at North American Aviation out at the Los Angeles International Airport, and their daughter, my little sister Carla, was two years old and needed someone to keep her from harming herself or anyone else while her parents were at work. I got that job. I was attending college in the mornings, but got home before Pop and Ethel went to work at four, so it was a good arrangement. Me and Carla got along fine. While I studied my homework in the living room, Carla would be taking care of business in the kitchen, maybe emptying out all the cabinets, dumping a pile of Ajax cleaner on the floor, and possibly mixing a family size box of oatmeal into it. To her, it looked like a pretty good sand pile to play in. To me, it looked like a headache.

Most things about that babysitting job I could handle pretty well. Carla was a cute little toddler with a mop of coal black hair and big brownish blue, green or gray or maybe black eyes. She was easy to get along with as long as I let her do anything she wanted to and gave her everything she wanted. It wasn't a bad arrangement. I could study or lie on the couch and watch TV while she played in a big mound of washing powder she had dumped on the carpet in the dining room. As long as she was quiet, my nerves stayed quiet.

I suppose I should qualify this on one point: the quiet, serene, peaceful time only started after Pop and Ethel left for work. She had them wrapped around her little finger, and would fret and fuss over the littlest things, like what color bowl she ate her cereal out of. She liked to wait until her mother filled her red bowl with milk and cereal before she whined for her blue bowl. Like me, Ethel figured the best way to handle her was to give the kid everything she wanted, and she would get the blue bowl down. While she filled it with milk and cereal, she would look up to see that Carla had already started eating the cereal in the red bowl. Stuff like that.

Carla always cried when her parents left for work (and it wasn't because they were leaving her with me! She just liked to control how things went). One day, Pop and Ethel were trying to leave for work, but Carla was squalling and clinging to Pop's leg so tight he couldn't dislodge her. He was shaking his leg and begging her to let go, and looked like he was almost ready to cry. "Son," he looked at me with a helpless, pleading eyes, "would you come over here and pull this kid off me?" So, I did, and she screamed and cried and threshed around until their car turned the corner and disappeared from sight. At that precise moment there was an instant transformation, like a switch had been turned off, and Carla was calm again, playing with her kittens and pushing her tricycle around the yard.

Getting her to sleep at night was the worst problem I had with Carla. College wasn't all that easy for me, being a flatland Tennessee boy caught out in movie star country crowded with more people than I would have believed the earth could hold. I needed to study at night, just so I could get through the next day's classes without embarrassing myself too badly. I cherished those two hours at night after I got Carla asleep before I went to bed myself. Sometimes she didn't want to go to sleep, and I had to get creative. One night I thought I had her down for the count, and I looked up from my textbook to see her standing in the doorway rubbing her eyes. It was dark in her room, and she wanted me to tell her a story. I put her back in her little bed and turned on a nightlight. I sat down beside her and told her a vampire story. I crept out when her eyes closed. I opened my book and resumed reading. I heard feet scuffling across the carpet and there she was. I rocked her to sleep, put her back in bed and tiptoed out. I found I couldn't concentrate on my studies anymore, anticipating her return from the dead yet again. And she didn't disappoint. When she entered the room the next time, I snapped.

I won't say I didn't feel like snatching her up and spanking her into submission, but I knew that wouldn't work. That kid was way too tough for that. That's when native cunning came to my aid. When my mama found out that us boys got too tough for a spanking to do any good, she got creative. She'd give us a dose of castor oil when we misbehaved. When we fought, she'd make us kiss and make up (just about the worst thing she could have done to two brothers who had just been seriously trying to kill each other). One thing she used a lot when she caught us doing something wrong was to make us keep doing it over and over until we got sick of it. She made my brother Jerry smoke cigars until he turned green one time after she caught him with a cigar stuck in his mouth, hoping to break him from smoking. That one didn't work, but it's one example of her unique style.

I thought it might work on Carla. I grabbed her little hand and we walked in a big circle around the living room. She thought it was a game, and skipped a little. We kept walking, and walking, and she looked up at me like, okay, that was fun, but when are we going to finish this game and go do something else? I kept her moving. I was getting tired myself, but I thought I detected a little lagging of her steps. We wore a path in the living room carpet, and I wouldn't be surprised if we wore the beads off the feet of her little footie pajamas. Anyway, it worked. When I realized I was dragging her, I picked the limp bundle up and took her to her bed. This time, she stayed put for the rest of the night.

The worst thing I ever did to Carla would today be classed as child abuse, no question. These days, I would go to jail for it. My only excuse is that I was a seventeen-year old male whose brain was not fully developed, and I was under terrific strain trying to adapt to living in a place that wasn't surrounded by woods. But I really have no excuse, because I blew up over something trivial.

I was at my usual studies and Carla was in her room playing. I could hear her moving around, but after a while I decided I needed to put eyes on her. I laid down my books and opened the door to her room to find clothes strewed all over everything. She was happily playing with something she had apparently been searching for. I picked up all the clothes and put them back in the drawers, and went back to study some more. A little later I went back to check on Carla and gasped when I saw the room more messed up than the first time. I fussed at the kid for trashing her room, put everything back in the drawers and went back to my books. A third time I checked on her, and this time it looked like she had been shopping at Goodwill and bought them out of their used clothing, just so she could bring it home to dump in her room to drive me nuts.

It worked. White specks flashed before my eyes. The room began to spin. I think my spirit left my body and ran out into the street to scream. Then an evil spirit came in and with crazed eyes and fangs bared, I descended on my cute, defenseless little sister, smiling up at me as if to say, look at what I did, all by myself. Hands twisted into claws, I grabbed her up and held her out a moment, not really seeing her. The drawers of her dresser were all open. I crammed her into the bottom one and slammed it shut, then stood back to gloat. The screams and sounds of beating on the drawer were soul satisfying. I think I drooled a little and rubbed my clawed hands together with glee. Then the evil spirit left, and I was myself again. Looking guiltily around, I opened the drawer to behold, not my baby sister, but two gigantic white eyes with tiny pinpoint pupils, and a mouth wide with screams. I picked her up and hugged her, and her arms around my neck almost choked me. Not one of my best days.

Okay, so my methods of raising kids may be a little unorthodox – not exactly what you get from these pencil neck psychologists and pediatricians, is it? But I'll have to say, Carla didn't turn out so bad. Whether it's because of my wonderful training or not, I don't know, but she sleeps all right now. After she looks under the bed, of course. Some people don't understand why she has the quilts over her bedroom windows, but I figure it's just her unique taste in decoration. Carla turned out to be a beautiful girl. People are always complimenting her on her big eyes. And they tell me that her stuttering is hardly noticeable any more.

All right, I guess this is all the help I can give you. I thought I should jot this stuff down in case you have found the books written by the egghead experts useless to help you with your kid. It may not be the best way to treat a difficult kid, and it may not even help them much...but it will give *you* a lot of satisfaction.

Tennessee Or Bust

June, 1958. I was living with my dad, Carl McCormick and my stepmother Ethel in Torrance, California. I had just completed my second year at El Camino College. I had seen all I wanted to see of Southern California for the time being, and was thinking how good it would be to see naturally growing green grass again. At the same time my brother Mick had just finished boot camp at the San Diego Naval Base and had hitched a ride up the coast to Torrance to see us before heading back to Tennessee on leave. He got me homesick enough until we made it up to drive back home in my car.

The thought never occurred to us that my car might not have three thousand miles left in it. It was a little metallic faded Prussian blue Ford coupe that Pop had bought for me to drive to school. I had just put in a set of rings and inserts, and the motor sounded all right to me. The crankshaft was pretty worn out, but I put in two or three sizes of rings, just to make sure I got a good fit somewhere. Maybe I wasn't much of a mechanic, but the thing ran, at least. At my age, and in my state of mind, I figured that's all we required.

Somehow my Uncle Rex got wind of our plans. His thirteen-year-old mama's boy, Leon, had been whining to go back east to spend the summer with grandma. Rex was overjoyed to find a free ride headed that way. It was all right with us. Leon was pretty skinny and wouldn't take up much room. A kid like that couldn't have much luggage. You could read relief all over Rex's face when we agreed to take Leon along. That should have told us something.

We got the car packed, and ended up with about a square foot of space in the back seat to play with. Pop must have been making some mental calculations, because just as I was wondering what we could cram into that tiny space, Pop snaps his fingers and goes, "Hey! I bet you could cram Jackie right into that spot!" Jackie Philip, our brother from Pop's second marriage, was about nine or ten, and had been shipped out to sunny California to spend his summer vacation with his dad. Now Pop saw his chance to ship him back.

"You boys won't mind Jackie riding along, will you?" Pop said, not waiting for an answer. "His mama's ready for him to come on home, and I wouldn't want to trust him on a bus…"

Didn't want to trust him on a *bus?* Anyway, we added one more to our passenger list. I never asked Pop and Rex about it, but I bet that summer went down as the peacefullest time they ever had. They got rid of all four of us boys in one fell swoop.

Unidentified Rolling Object

The day came for us to pull out. The car was already packed, but we added a car top carrier and piled it about four feet high with last minute stuff we suddenly realized we couldn't do without. The trunk was full. We had included pretty much everything except the stopper for the Pacific Ocean. And we were only carrying the bare necessities. I knew I would be needing those two antique leather-bound tomes of Shakespeare that I had bought in a pawn shop for five dollars apiece. Together they wouldn't weigh over forty pounds. I was taking a big block of solid walnut that I wanted to carve something out of sooner or later, and a few oil paintings I had done in class, so I could show the folks back home what I'd been learning.

Mick had his sea bag full of dirty clothes, but nothing else, except a pack of Kools he had swiped off Pop's dresser.

It was Leon who showed me that I had no imagination at all when it came to packing only those items that were absolutely necessary to the trail.

Leon was bringing his scooter. You know…a scooter, like you stand on with one foot and push with the other. And he couldn't do without his basketball, fully inflated. I didn't recognize everything Leon threw in, but I wasn't going to let him outdo me. I wedged my guitar in. Now we were prepared for any possible emergency. A body never knows when he's liable to be needing a basketball, or a guitar, or his scooter.

Jackie...I don't remember him taking anything along but the clothes on his back.

By the time we all got in, the old Ford was hunkered down so low that one of my sister Carla's kittens couldn't have crawled underneath. The running boards scraped the curb as we eased out into Steveanne Street. I wrestled the wheel around and got the car pointed in the right direction before I looked back over my shoulder to take a last look at my California home.

The picture is printed forever in my memory – the basic pink stucco tract home with garage, in this case overflowing with old TVs, radios and other junk Pop collected to tinker with while learning electronics by home correspondence course. I remember the weed box underneath the kitchen window (no flowers would ever grow there). The family was standing on the sidewalk waving goodbye. My three-year-old sister Carla had one of her luckless little kittens by its stubby little tail, idly kicking it in the head to make it swing while she waved bye-bye with the other little brown hand. Pop wore a combination worried/relieved expression as he watched us creep away. My stepmother Ethel was shaking her head at the moving mountain of machinery, boys and junk. She was mumbling to herself, "They'll never make it...they'll never make it."

Blinking back a tear, I faced resolutely ahead, took a firm grip on the steering wheel and floorboarded it. A little kid eating a popsicle whizzed past us on roller-skates. His backwash rocked our car. I held the gas pedal down, and gradually we drew even with the next-door neighbor's house. We were picking up steam. We caught up with the kid on skates and passed him. The car strained ahead as I shifted into second gear, and we were on our way.

An hour later we were still fighting traffic through town when Jackie says, "Are we there yet?" Leon says, "I gotta use the bathroom." And Mick says…well, maybe I better not say what Mick said.

As it worked out, we had to stop anyway, because the car quit on us. One minute we're rolling along, and then suddenly the motor just dies. We coasted into a service station that happened to be handy, and the guy there checked under the hood. He informed us that we had us a vapor lock. I thought he was making some kind of crack about our intelligence or something, and commenced to get mad. But he explained that a vapor lock had something to do with overheating, so that the gas would vaporize before it got into the carburetor, or something. When that happened, he said, we had two options; we could either pour cold water on the fuel pump, or we could just sit and wait for it to cool off. Then the car would start, and everything would be hunky-dory. Until it overheated again. No big deal. It didn't happen too often, and we needed to stop and rest every now and then anyway. We'd definitely get there sooner or later, maybe.

Little by little we made it out of town without the cops stopping us. Not that we were speeding or anything. We were more like, obstructing traffic. I guess the cops figured it was better to go ahead and allow us to escape from their jurisdiction rather than to try to describe our vehicle in their report.

The Urge to Kill

The day began to heat up as we moved out into the arid open spaces of the California desert. We stopped to gas up and recharge our "air conditioner." I'm just trying to be funny about the air conditioner. Auto air conditioners were not standard equipment in those days. We had to invent our own method of cooling off. What we did was go in the bathroom at each service station we stopped at, take off our tee shirts and soak them in the sink. Without wringing the water out we'd put the shirts back on, run jump in the car and sizz off with the vent windows turned in on us. That was good for no more than five or ten miles of semi-relief before the hot desert air sucked the shirts dry. The only problem with our makeshift "air conditioner" was that it blew hot air.

It was definitely *hot*. This was the Southern California desert we had around us, an area often listed as the hottest place in the country. The few cars we met on that lonely stretch of highway seemed to float three feet above the pavement, riding the shimmering heat waves. They connected to the highway again as they drew closer. About every five minutes Jackie would pop his favorite question: "Are we there yet?"

"Good grief, Jackie! This is the Mo-havvie Desert! Just take a look around…does this look like Tennessee to you, huh?"

The first flush of excitement and adventure was definitely beginning to wear off.

We labored up a long incline crossing the San Gabriel Mountains, the motor straining to pull the weight of us and our stuff. We almost made it to the top when the gas vaporized again. We pulled over on the shoulder of the road and got out. The world suddenly became very quiet. I had never been anywhere as quiet as it was out there, far from city or farm. Far from people. I doubted if even animals could live in that heat. I sure didn't see any.

I imagined I could hear sand settling. When I listened closely the silence was more like a faint whisper, or a long sigh drifting across the desert. The view was endless. League upon league of grey sand, rock and cactus. We had somehow managed to have a stall out smack in the middle of a vast, empty land, with nothing in sight to encourage the heart as far as help was concerned. There was absolutely no traffic in sight either way. We could see probably twenty miles of our back trail, but not a speck appeared. A body could have laid down right there in the middle of that blacktop highway and taken a nap...only they would have found themselves fried to death when they woke up! Wasn't much danger of being run over though.

When we had gotten out of the car the radiator was hissing, so Mick went to loosen the cap to let off some pressure. The cap was blistering hot when he touched it, so he raised his foot to kick it loose. The sole of that shoe was all that saved him from a blistering steam job. When he kicked it loose, the radiator cap blew off and a geyser of boiling water sprayed against the bottom of Mick's shoe. He was smart enough to keep his big foot in place against the spout, deflecting the steam until the geyser died down. When it stopped, there wasn't even a gurgle left in the radiator. Every single drop of water must have boiled out or evaporated.

That took care of one idea that I had been toying with. I had read somewhere that if you got stranded on the desert without water you could drink radiator water after it cooled, in a life-or-death emergency. And this was shaping up to look like a sure enough emergency.

Not that I figured we would actually have to depend on the radiator water to drink. We had a jug of ice water for that, in a big gallon thermos. We had set it out on the fender, figuring to pour some of it into the radiator when it cooled down enough. While we waited I walked out on the desert a ways, to have a look around and stretch my legs a bit.

"Boys," I said, "this here is some real desert! Just look at all that sand, and all them cactuses..."

I was interrupted by a dull "thunk" behind me, and I turned. Leon was standing beside the fender of the car, wiping his mouth with the tail of his shirt. He was looking down at the thermos jug, lying there at his feet, cap off, spilling the last of its precious contents in the thirsty sand.

"Leon!" I screamed, "that's the last of our water, you ninny!" Suddenly the emergency aspect of our situation took center stage. Forget adding enough water in the radiator to get us going again. Forget my Boy Scout idea about drinking radiator water. My mouth was already dry as cotton. I began having visions of bones in the sand…

"Well, shoot," Leon drawled, "I was just gettin' myself a drink, and the blame jug slipped. Ain't no big deal anyway. We'll just stop and fill the dang jug at the next fillin' station."

"Leon…." I was trying hard to hold my temper. "Leon, do you *see* any fillin' stations out there?" I swung my arm in a wide arc, taking in the empty landscape. "Do you see *anything* out there? We ain't seen a sign of a car since we stopped. And here we are in the middle of the Mo-havvie Desert with a dry radiator, a dry water jug, and unless there is something close over on the other side of that hill, this here junk heap ain't agonna make it to no fillin' station!"

I had to remind myself that you don't just arbitrarily kick the slats out of kids littler than you, even if they are your idiot cousin.

The buzzard that landed on a big rock beside the road didn't make me feel any better about our situation, either.

We decided to try pushing the car to the top of the hill and coast as far as possible down the other side. Maybe we'd see a place to get some water before we had to start the engine again. But when we stopped to rest at the top of the hill, things didn't look too encouraging. As far as the eye could see there were only dancing heat waves. No service station. No house. No human. No car. Even the highway seemed to just disappear into a blue haze. Up the creek didn't seem to be the appropriate phrase for that desert, but the sentiment was the same.

We estimated the downgrade to be about five miles long, so that was hopeful. Maybe we would find something somewhere in all that haze down in the valley. We put the car in neutral, pushed it off and jumped in. The coasting was fine while it lasted, but it didn't last long, and we didn't see so much as a ditch with water in it. Finally, I had to turn on the ignition and throw her in second gear. The motor caught, and I eased the little coupe along the floor of the valley, watching the heat gage climb. We rolled past some barns that had been hidden from view by the haze, but there was no sign of a house, or any life. We didn't see anything that looked like cattle watering tubs or even a bucket. Nothing.

By this time the motor had gotten about as hot as it could get. The heat needle had probably made three revolutions and the motor was making a sound like shaking a washtub full of gravel. Then we topped out on a little rise and suddenly found ourselves at the junction of Route 66. We had made it to Barstow. There at the intersection, like a beautiful mirage, was a wonderful little service station. I breathed a sigh of relief and pulled in to the pump. We had everything filled to capacity with gas, oil and above all, water. We also filled ourselves to capacity with soft drinks. We could hear our stomachs sloshing as we walked back to the car and got in.

Details of the next leg of our journey are foggy in my memory. I don't, for instance, remember eating anything on the entire trip, but undoubtedly we did, or Mick would have died. We drove through the night. When my eyes began to cross, Mick took the wheel and I slept, sitting up in the passenger seat. We crossed Arizona that night. The next morning, I was driving somewhere in New Mexico, trying to convince myself that the motor didn't sound any worse than it did when we left Barstow. I traded with Mick again and slept while he drove. Leon and Jackie could sleep anytime they wanted to, which was most of the time. We began to feel like some kind of crop, grown to the car.

Culture Comes To Moriarty, New Mexico

The sound of wheels crunching on loose gravel snapped me out of a deep sleep. The car rolled to a stop as I sat up, wiping my sandpapery face with a gritty palm. On the second try to make sound come out of my throat I was able to mumble, "Whereizzis?"

"Bleepfino," Mick replied. "Someplace name of 'Garage,' according to the sign."

I straightened myself up and looked around. Mick had parked in front of a squat concrete block building surrounded by dust covered junk cars. A big sign over the door said "Garage."

A homely man of considerable bulk, dressed in greasy overalls lumbered out of a doorway and slouched over to our car. "Do sump'n' for you boys?" he inquired around a cheek full of cut plug.

"See can you tell me what's the matter with this motor, will you?" Mick said, and goosed the gas pedal. I can't do sound effects on paper, but in English it sounded something like this: *Wraaghclacketyclacketywhopety whop BAM!*

The old mechanic didn't even bother to look under the hood. He leaned a massive forearm on the car windowsill and spat tobacco juice on the gravel. "She's a-fixin' to th'ow a rod, son," he said.

"How much to fix it?"

The mechanic scratched his grizzled head. "'Fraid I couldn't get to it for a couple of days, boys. What you're gonna need is a new block."

A new block. *A whole new motor?* Mick did some quick calculations. "How much you gimme for this fine car?"

The mechanic chuckled. "Well, son, I already got more junk cars parked around this place than I need. But you can leave her settin' here until you come back through if you like."

Me and Mick looked at one another. We really didn't plan on dropping back through Flyspeck, New Mexico any time soon. Mick asked where we were and directions to the nearest bus station, and learned that the proper name of the place was Moriarty. While Mick drove off to check on the price of bus tickets, me and the boys went inside the garage to wait. On a whim I decided to take my paintings in with me. I knew we'd never get all our junk on a bus, and were going to have to leave some of it behind. This old mechanic was being helpful to us,

83

and he sized up like a man who might have good taste. I decided I would bequeath my priceless masterpieces to him.

When I walked inside and saw his wife leaning against the counter, I revised my opinion somewhat regarding that wrench jockey's good taste. That woman filled out a dirty black sweater like three hundred pounds of lumpy cotton in a four-foot sack. She gapped a smile at us boys when we came in, and patted her hair. I had a bad minute trying to keep my stomach settled. It was just too early in the morning for a sight like that.

"You fellers come right on in and set, and have a sody," she invited. I noticed her eying the canvases her husband was leaning up against the wall. I was reaching in the drink box for a cold drink, but out of the corner of my eye I caught her reaction to one of the paintings. Her thick eyebrows went up and she jobbed her husband in the ribs with her elbow.

"Looky, Clarence," she whispered loudly, and nodded to the painting on the end. "That there's a *nekked* woman, Clarence!"

The proper name usually applied to that genre of painting is "nude." But I was of no mind to be correcting a lady who was offering us a bit of hospitality.

I made Clarence and the wife a gift of my paintings rather than try to wag them along on a bus. Probably if I had gone around in back and dumped the paintings in the trash I could have saved Clarence the trouble of doing it later, but this way I could at least pretend my masterpieces would find a good home with these fine, cultured folks.

Goodbye To The Car – But Not To The Scooter

We heard Mick come rolling up outside. A big cloud of yellow dust rolled up with him. He got out of the car waving a twenty-dollar bill. "I sold her," he said.

"Sold who?" I said.

"I sold the car, dang it!"

"For *twenty dollars?*" I squawked.

"Price of a bus ticket home – for you. I got enough for me and Leon. Jackie has enough left out of what Pop gave him." Leave It to Mick to have all the angles figured. He seemed pleased at the turn of events. "From here on," he said with satisfaction, we leave the driving to someone else."

The first thing Mick had done when he got to the bus station (which also housed the local post office, as well as a convenience store and a restaurant) was to ask if anyone knew where he could sell a car. The proprietor, as it happened, had been looking around for a set of wheels for his teenage son. He stepped outside to take a look. Mick got in and spun the little Ford around in the loose gravel a couple of times, and concluded the sale. At a price the guy couldn't refuse. But I don't figure we took too bad a fleecing. Pop didn't give but $35 for the old clunker to begin with.

We could have had a yard sale with the items we left in the car or threw away. I chose to leave everything but my guitar, books and clothes. Leon refused to part with anything except his basketball, which he punctured with his pocketknife rather than give it to some poor little Indian kid. We pled with him to leave that moronic scooter. Mick even offered to buy it from Leon, so he could junk it, but Leon stubbornly declined. For the second time me and Mick looked at each other and considered whether it would be right to leave Leon *and* his stupid scooter with the unsuspecting folks of this friendly little town.

But we finally got ourselves divested of extra weight, so we could travel light – all except for Leon – and when that big air-conditioned Greyhound bus pulled out of Moriarty, New Mexico, we were all four on board, our dusty carcasses sprawled in luxury on deep cushions. I don't know what the others did for the first hundred miles. I slept.

When I finally came to, I sat up and took stock. Jackie and Leon lay stretched out asleep on the back seat that went across the width of the bus. I stretched and scratched, relishing the feel of a dry shirt. It was nice on that bus. We didn't have to soak our shirts and roll a window down to stay cool. Man, I could live on this thing! It was only the second long bus ride of my life. I had no idea how luxurious a ride could be.

Three or four seats ahead of me, Mick had found another sailor boy to sit with, both of them dressed in their navy-blue sailor suits. They were smoking and talking (in those days smoking was permitted on a bus). I noticed the other guy look over his shoulder and nod his head in my direction. He said something to Mick and laughed. Mick flicked the ash off the end of his cigarette and nodded agreement. I couldn't hear his reply.

Mick filled me in later, when we went in to eat at the next rest stop.

He and the other sailor had been talking abut where each other was from. When Mick said he was from Tennessee, near Memphis, it made the other guy think of Elvis, who was just getting to be popular at that time.

But let me pause here to give you an idea of how I looked when I got on that bus. I was tall and skinny, with dust streaming from my clothes. I had a beatup guitar slung over one shoulder and, I'm ashamed to admit, long hair. Collar length hair, and it was going in all directions. And this was before the days of the hippies. It was just that I didn't like barbers, and hadn't been sighted by one for over two years. Let me put it this way…if I stood on one leg I looked like the kitchen mop.

So, this other sailor says to Mick, "Speaking of Elvis, have you noticed that bushy-headed so-and-so (not the actual word he said) sitting in the back?"

"Yeah," Mick agrees fervently, flicking the ash off his cigarette. "Looks like the devil (not the actual word he said), don't he?"

And him my own brother.

We got off the bus at Little Rock, Arkansas, and called our sister Ramona. She and her husband Ralph were stationed at the Air Force base in Jacksonville. Mona came and got us and took us to her house to spend the night. You'd have thought we had come back from the dead, the way Mona took on over seeing us again, and when I laid eyes on her and Ralph and the kids, I began to feel like I was home.

Wake Up Call

Mona made pallets on the floor for us that night. It sure felt better than droning through the hot desert night with your hands grown to a steering wheel and your eyes about ready to turn backwards in your head. Not even the excitement of being reunited with family could keep me awake that night.

I awoke at the crack of dawn the next morning. I was sure it was the crack of dawn, because I heard it crack. However, when I opened my eyes all I could see was a bunch of red and purple and yellow neon stars flying around, so I thought it must still be night. I blinked my eyes a couple of times and the stars gradually faded away. I became aware that I was lying on my back on the floor, looking up at the ceiling, and it was broad daylight.

I heard a guttural baby chuckle, and looked back over my head. There stood Bobby, who was Mona's baby at the time. The happy little toddler was wearing a soggy diaper and swinging a baby bottle by the nipple, rocking back and forth from one fat little bare foot to the other. He was drooling a big, wide grin. When he saw me open my eyes, he squatted and raised his bottle over his head, holding it by the nipple. Then he brought his bottle of milk down hard with both hands – right in the center of my forehead. It connected with a sound not unlike the busting of a ripe watermelon over your knee, and suddenly it went night again.

When I finally fought my way back to consciousness Bobby was gone, thank God. I guess he figured I was too hard to wake up.

I recovered in time to make it to the table for breakfast, and then Mona loaded us up in her car for the final run into Tennessee. When we crossed the Mississippi River bridge at Memphis and saw that sign halfway over that said, "Tennessee State Line," me and Mick straightened everybody's hair with a wild rebel yell. Dog if I had *ever* seen so much green trees and grass in my life as I saw along that river bank.

That night the little house at Five Points where we grew up was alive with the sounds of laughter and conversation. After Mama had made over us and fed us, we sat up late bringing each other up to date on all the news. I had to tell them all about California and college. Then, while Mick regaled them with stories of Navy life, I went outside, closing the screen door softly behind me. The cool night air felt good to my flushed face. I breathed deep of the smell of the woods. Somewhere in their shadowy depths a whippoorwill called. I strolled out to the edge of the road and leaned against the old silverleaf tree. I stood there a long time, unthinking, just looking out into the endless night. For two years I had not been out of sight of millions of electric lights that never went out. Out here in the country, for as far as I could see, except for the house behind me, not a single light broke the darkness. Only the stars.

Only the stars…

I felt a long pent-up tension begin to ease, like a slowly released breath. Something peaceful turned over inside me and fell comfortably into place.

I was home.

I turned my face up to the starry sky and let the grateful tears come, burning the tiredness from my eyes.

My First Big City Job Interview

You'd think that after living in Los Angeles County, California, in the All-American city of Torrance, that a Tennessee country boy would have learned a little more sophistication than I did. What I did out there wasn't what I'd call really living anyway. What I did mostly was breathe smog, eat, sleep, study and stay in the house minding my own business. Everybody out there talked with an accent. I never did learn how to get along.

Eventually, I made it back to Tennessee, and I have not been back since. California ain't home. Tennessee is. If you want to talk to me about going back to California, you're going to have to burn the woods and sift the ashes to find me. What a relief it was to get back out into fresh air, air I couldn't see.

Back in Tennessee, I laid around for about a year, eating my mother out of house and home. I didn't even look for a job. After my mama dropped enough hints, I finally decided I'd ease her mind a little. My buddy, Buford Ellington, was fixing to go down to Memphis to look for a job, so I thought I'd just ride along with him, so she'd think I was looking for a job too. After we got there I figured I might as well go ahead and take a shot at job hunting. We stayed with friends for a few days while we pounded the pavement. Buford didn't land a job that trip, but I made a contact that would eventually work out to be my first job in the art profession. Later on, Bue tried again and got a job in Memphis, and we got a room together in a fleabag flop house. We stayed there a week, reasonably satisfied until the landlady put an old man in the room with us who snored. He was a retired railroad man, and when he snored it sounded like one of his steam locomotives. We couldn't sleep with him snorting all night, so we left. We weren't eating any too well at that place anyway. Most mornings, before we could wash up and get to the table, the roaches would have already eaten half our breakfast. That's the place where we learned how to eat raisin pie. First, we'd stick a fork in the pie and wait, giving the raisins time to crawl off. When everything quit moving, it was safe to eat.

We went from there to a good boarding house, a nice, clean place serving two good meals a day. But we soon got lonesome for the roaches, and wound up renting our own fleabag duplex apartment. I used to have dreams about that place. The roaches there were bigger, and they had names. They were identifiable. One of them, Maurice, had this tattoo...

Well, never mind that. On that first day of job hunting, me and Bue, we started out downtown at some employment agency on Madison Avenue. The first thing they did was ask us what we thought we could do, then they called around and got us some appointments with companies that they thought we could do it to. The way it worked was, if we made any money we were supposed to split it with the employment agency. That seemed pretty reasonable to a couple of country boys who had no idea how to pick up a phone and make an appointment, especially since we didn't have any telephone.

We lit out afoot, headed east. We decided that when we'd come to one of the addresses they'd given us we'd both go in. I'd go in with Buford and sit around in my suit while he had his interview, and he'd go in with me and sit around in his suit while I had my interview. The thing is, my first appointment was all the way out on Poplar Avenue, almost to Highland. After we'd walked about five miles Buford had an appointment in another direction, so we went ahead and split up. Looking back, I wonder sometimes if maybe Buford had gotten a little tired of all the footwork and decided to take in a picture show or spend the rest of the afternoon at the zoo. Neither of us had been paying any attention to the big city buses that swooshed by, or to the signs that said, "Bus Stop." We just kept hoofing along, minding our own business and allowing those bus drivers to do the same. After Bue dropped off I went on alone. I had an address on a little slip of paper, and I was checking street numbers as I went along. I had a ways to go.

I probably hadn't walked more than 300 blocks, or maybe ten miles, when I noticed the street numbers getting in range of the number I had on the paper. Then, there it was… 3329 Poplar. Simon & Gwynn Advertising, just like it said on the paper.

Memphis was a lot bigger than the woods behind my house in Five Points, but I had followed the trail to the place I was looking for just from the scribblings the agency lady had put down for me. *I ain't as dumb as I look*, I says to myself, with a smug little smile on my face.

Taking a deep breath, I tucked the paper away in a pocket and coasted on in.

The swinging glass door swished shut behind me and the girl behind the receptionist's desk looked up. She looked again. What she saw didn't seem to match some kind of pattern she had in her mind. There I stood, six foot one, a hundred and fifty-five pounds, wearing an eighty dollar suit that I had saved up and bought for occasions like this, when I wanted to impress folks. Maybe that suit did look a little like it was hanging from a coat hanger instead of a body, but I thought the store had done a good job of taking up the pants. They had taken enough slack out of the waist of those pants so that the pockets met in the back. But the salesman had assured me that was the coming style. So, I was proud to be standing there, a trend setter.

My skinny red neck poked out of a starched collar two sizes too big, and my hair was slicked back with Vitalis, which was running down the side of my head along with the sweat. I had on a pair of borrowed regulation black US Navy shoes that my uncle Ben had worn at Pearl Harbor during World War Two, with white socks, rolled down to the shoe tops, Five Points,Tennessee style. I stood there before that receptionist's admiring eyes, not surprised at all by her speechlessness. I knew she was probably hesitating while trying to think of some flattering remark to throw me off guard.

Before she got a chance to put in her two cents, I threw out my chest and spoke right up.

"I'd like to see Mister, uh...." I fished the paper out of my pocket again and glanced at it. "Uh, Mister Gordon," I said. "Mr. Gordon, please." I thought I sounded awfully professional.

"Cert – certainly, sir," the girl stammered, reaching for the phone. I noticed she kept looking at me out of the corner of her eye. Never seen anybody like me before, I realized, reaching to straighten my tie. Why – the dadgum thing had come loose and was hanging off the first button of my coat! Danged bothersome...

"Uh – what's that, ma'am?"

"I said, who are you with, sir?" the girl asked, holding one hand over the intercom phone.

Now, what kind of question was that? I took a glance behind me, first over one shoulder, then over the other. There was nobody else in the room.

"Why – nobody, ma'am," I said gently. The poor girl was either seeing things or needed glasses. "I'm by myself, "Ma'am."

That girl managed to announce me to Mr. Gordon and got me directed through the building to his office, but she sure made a mess of it. She kept choking over her words, like, "Carlos, choke – I've got a live one – gasp – I mean...a gentleman out

95

here – gurgle, choke..." and stuff like that. Why, if I'd been the big shot who owned that company I'd of never hired a girl who stuttered to sit at the front desk to answer the phone and meet the public.

If I get a job here, I says to myself, *I'll have to coach this girl how to be more sophisticated*. As I strutted confidently down the hall to my interview, I thought it was cool how the straw and manure from my shoes blended so nicely with the green carpet.

I worked that job six years.

Test Driver

My brother Mick was a great guy with a heart as big as a dairy barn. And sometimes he was full of the same kind of stuff you're likely to find on the floor of a dairy barn.

Mick worked in Memphis. A buddy of his at work was trying to sell him his car, a little yellow Volkswagen. One day after work, Mick took it for a test drive. He eased it through the rush hour traffic and headed for open country. Out on the highway he put the pedal to the metal and gave her the acid test. At high speed he had a little trouble holding the car steady. Mick was a pretty big guy, about six feet tall. He filled that VW so that his elbows were sticking out both side windows. His right knee kept knocking the rearview mirror out of line. He was an accident going someplace to happen.

When Mick failed to show up for supper, his wife Joyce went to the window to see if the world had come to an end. She checked the clock in the kitchen and confirmed that the boy had made history. In all their years together, Mick had never missed feeding time.

Joyce studied on it for a few minutes, then on an impulse grabbed her car keys and cigarettes. Maybe it would be a good idea to just drive up and down and check on some of the dives along the highway.

Just as she was about to pull out onto the main drag, a patrol car zoomed by, siren wailing. Some premonition told Joyce to follow the trooper. She hadn't gone far when she met an ambulance headed back in the opposite direction, emergency lights flashing. That didn't do much for her peace of mind. A little further down the road she saw the smokey, parked behind another patrol car. A crowd had gathered, looking down at something hidden from sight by the shoulder of the road. Joyce parked her car and got out, her hands already beginning to tremble, afraid of what she might see. She elbowed through the crowd and looked over in the ditch.

Judging from the amount of scrap metal, what she saw there looked like it could have been one of those little foreign imports, possibly a VW. She turned a pale face to the cop standing there and asked him what happened.

"Feller lost control of his vehicle," he said, rolling a wad of chewing tobacco into another cheek. "We cut the poor sucker out of that mess and sent him to the hospital in the meat wagon. He wasn't dead, but his face looked like King Kong and Mighty

Joe Young had used it for the bird in a badminton game – the operative word bein' *bad*."

The cop spat into the grass. "I.D. says the dude's name was T.M. McCormick."

The cop had to reach out suddenly to steady Joyce on her feet. "You all right, ma'am?" he asked with concern. She had started bawling, fumbling through the clutter in her purse. "I - I can't – snarf – can't find my cigarettes," she blubbered.

The officer scratched his head.

Mick came to in the emergency room, and about all he could move was his mouth. He opened one owl eye and got it focused on the nurse who was bending over him picking pieces of dashboard out of his face. She was black.

As I said, there was nothing wrong with Mick's mouth, unfortunately. He looked at the girl and cracked, "You ain't half bad for a n---" That's as far as he got before a ragged piece of plastic was forcibly reinserted into the cut from which it had just been extracted. Joyce said she never heard a better scream.

Miraculously, not a bone was broken. Nor were there any internal injuries. However, if a single muscle in Mick's body escaped being bruised, pulled or otherwise traumatized, it failed to show up in the next few days. Mick couldn't even turn over in bed by himself. A fly making a rough landing on him would bring a grimace of pain. He got so stiff that if he'd had any broken bones he would have been his own splints.

But his mouth, of course, never slowed down. He livened the place up so that all the nurses got to taking their breaks in his room. They still allowed smoking in hospital rooms in those days, and the smoke would sometimes get so thick that Mick wouldn't even have to light up. All he had to do was just inhale. Joyce would just sit there and roll her eyes as Mick started in on some outlandish yarn. When I went by to visit, the room was filled with folks, most of whom I didn't know. Mick didn't know them all either. A lot of them just dropped in to hear some fresh material.

Well, Mick got so fresh with some of the nurses that they up and discharged him before he was really able to get around by himself. Typical of his wit was the comment he made to me on my last visit:

"Joe, I've gave a lot of thought to it," he said, "and I've decided not to buy that blamed Volkswagen. I don't like the way it handles."

Kicking A Rat

Summer is an endless time in the inner city. Asphalt and concrete drink up the scorching sunlight during the long, smoky days, and retain its heat long after the sun has burnt itself out beyond the red horizon. In the evenings after supper you can hear screen doors slam softly and porch swings creak as neighbors come out for a quiet smoke or a glass of iced tea, hoping for a refreshing breeze. Here and there sweaty children play catch-the-bug under the street lights. The humidity bears down, frustrating sleep until the cool night breezes begin. At such times young men grow restless, defiant of any threat to their need for violent activity.

Under these conditions a rat who is unfortunate enough to let himself be seen crossing a parking lot is no longer a simple, law-abiding rodent out for a leisurely evening stroll. He becomes instead a welcome diversion.

In the summer of 1961, Buford Ellington and I shared a fleabag duplex apartment on Watkins Street in midtown Memphis. Two of our old schoolmates, Horace and his brother Ralph, had also come to the big city to make their fortunes, and had taken lodging with their sister in another fleabag apartment across the street from us at the corner of Peach Avenue. We usually hung out together at night, either at their place or ours, lolling around on the overgrown lawn, getting chiggers and shooting the breeze. We had us a car, but nowhere to go.

One sultry night as we sat there chewing grass stems and bragging, Ralph suddenly sat up straight, craning his neck toward the parking lot across the street.

"Whatcha see," Bue asked. Not that it would have made any difference. Anything at all was worth checking out if it offered the slightest possibility of variety.

"Dono," Ralph mumbled. "Looks like prob'ly a rat or sump'n, maybe." You never dealt in specifics when you dealt with Ralph.

We all stood up and looked. Sure enough, there he was, right smack in the middle of the dimly lit parking lot, shuffling along like he was in no particular hurry. Maybe he had just finished off a huge garbage soufflé, perhaps washing it down with a nice brown sewer wine at his favorite dump. We could just imagine him ambling along, a toothpick between his teeth, burping occasionally as he enjoyed the rotten pizza and fish scales all over again.

He stood out like a sitting duck in the green glow of the street lights on the parking lot. Something about the repulsive shape appealed to the murderous side of our nature. The gorge rose up in our throats. The minute we caught sight of that scuzzball his doom was sealed. Nobody likes a rat.

We stampeded across the street yelling, "Get a stick!" and, "Don't let him get away!" and, "Wait until you see his face... It might be somebody we know!"

When he looked up and spotted us bearing down on him like a herd of elephants, the rat halted and stood his ground, eyeing us carefully one at a time. He was a big dude. His dirty brown fur was all matted and scruffy, like he'd been in a barroom brawl or something. He cocked his head first to this side and then to that side, as if he were seriously weighing his chances of taking on all four of us at once. Suddenly I was very glad there were three other guys out on that parking lot with me and that tough looking rat.

Apparently deciding against a head-on attack, the rat began to waddle (he probably called it running) toward the nearest clump of bushes. Ralph was there before him with a stick to head him off. Ol' Ralph's heavy-lidded eyes widened when he got closer up to our ferocious looking friend. The thing made like he was going to run right between Ralph's legs. Uttering a high-pitched maniacal shriek, Ralph let fly with his mightiest home-run swing. The length of two-by-two he was carrying almost broke in two as it connected with brother rat's bloated paunch. The rodent was flung back to the center of the empty lot, and we all closed in for the kill.

Our luckless victim picked himself up and shook his head. His beady eyes cut this way and that. Then he made a quick dash toward Horace. Bad move. Horace wears a size thirteen shoe, and one of them came down on that rat like an upside-down aircraft carrier. It was like stomping on a ball of rubber. The rat was addled, but he wasn't out. Horace drew back and gave him a powerful kick that sent the hideous thing skidding across the asphalt toward me. I let out a startled yell and began kicking insanely three or four times before the furry projectile even rolled into range. Then my toe connected, and I punted the filthy ball of slime through the air in Buford's direction. Bue almost panicked, thinking he was going to get the thing right in the face. He threw his hands up in front. But instead the rat bounced off his knee and ol' Bue did a frenzied jitterbug on the poor ol' guy's body.

Then for a little while it was open season on that rat. We chased and kicked and yelled and chunked until our rodent friend could hardly drag his repulsive carcass across the ground. We all converged on him at once and got in a tangle, almost killing each other trying to kick the snot out of that ugly rat. Somebody's shoe took a strip of hide off my shinbone. My elbow got Horace in the goozle as I was jumping to avoid those vicious yellow teeth.

Finally, we backed off to get our breath. The sweat dripped from our red faces, and our T-shirts were plastered to our heaving sides. Cautiously, we eyed the bag of fur stretched out motionless on the asphalt, looking for any sign of life.

"Reckin we done killed 'im?" Buford queried.

But no – as we watched, incredulously the raggedy lump stirred, staggered to its feet and stood, swaying unsteadily, trying to get its eyes focused.

"That – that beats anything I ever seen!" Horace breathed with awe.

I agreed. That pointy-faced rat had taken everything we could throw at him, and still he could pick himself up, brush himself off and glare at us like he was deciding whether we'd had enough or if he should take us on again.

I don't like rats. Don't believe in 'em. But I just couldn't help feeling a little tug of admiration wrung out of me as that beady-eyed bag of fur turned, having decided to let us off, and lurched drunkenly off into the darkness.

We let him go. Just as he faded into the deep shadows I'm sure I heard a distinct burp.

The night had grown almost imperceptibly cooler. We hung around a little longer, fanning our T-shirts out away from our bodies, laughing and telling each other every detail of what we had just been doing, like it was news or something. A June bug droned past and dinged himself off a light post. Gradually we wound down and began to yawn and scratch. A little breeze was beginning to stir. The sleeping ought to be good now, with a window raised.

"C'mon, Ralph, let's hit the sack," Horace said, getting to his feet.

"Well, see y'all tomorrow."

"Bye."

"Take it easy."

Soon the cooling parking lot was empty again, but nobody was there to know.

The following night, and for several nights after that, we kept looking hopefully over at the parking lot, but we never saw that mangy rat again. We felt regret at his absence, but I doubt if he missed us. At least he had been a lot more fun than hanging around the telephone booth and waiting for the phone to ring, or something.

We conducted a half-hearted search through the bushes and leaves, thinking maybe we had really done the scudder in, but we never found a body. We did find, however, a crumpled map of Memphis, with rat tracks on it. Near the Yacht Club at Mud Island, at the point where the Mississippi River barges tie up, there was a red circle marked.

Sadly, we concluded that our rat buddy figured it was time to ship out to friendlier climates, to someplace where there would be no kicks coming over a rat moving into the neighborhood.

Whupped With A Butcher Knife

I guess I was a little past twenty when this happened to me. I had me a job with an advertising agency in Memphis, and with my first money I went and made a down payment on a motorcycle. It was a BSA, made in Birmingham, England, and don't ask me all the technical details, because I'm not really a motorcycle nut. I couldn't tell you anything about the cylinder, cc's or sprocketwhatzit. All I cared was that I thought I would look cool sitting up on that thing wearing a pair of aviator sunglasses with my hair blowing in the wind. I can say that it was a used bike with two wheels that looked okay, one headlight, one tail light and a kick starter. Leo, the dealer, assured me the title was all right, though I later suspected it was not when I couldn't find the VIN number. But what did I care about titles? It sounded good when I revved her up, and I slung gravel in Leo's face when I peeled off the lot.

I may have already recounted the story of my first road trip on the BSA, so I won't go back over how I had to learn that there was more to riding a motorcycle than just sitting up there on top of it looking cool in sunglasses. After my first near-death experience I learned how to handle the thing, and loved how it felt to ride in the open air. It was my only mode of transportation, and I usually took it out into the country every weekend. Up and down the hills, sailing around curves, horses coming out to race me down the fence line as I passed...I loved it.

One weekend I left work early on Friday and took off to visit my family in Five Points, over in Madison County. It was about a two-hour trip. It was summertime, and hot. Somewhere along the way I stopped and took off my tee shirt, shook the bugs out of it and tied it around my waist. My hair was pretty long and stood out in all directions (we seldom wore helmets in those days), but I made sure the shades were in place. By the time I got to Mom's house I was hot and tired, my lower back stiff and sore, and I had a case of nerves from the road noise and tension left over from my job. I pulled into the driveway, cut off the engine, set the kickstand and got off the motorcycle, grateful for the sudden quiet. I had to straighten the fingers of my right hand, which had been clamped onto the accelerator handle of the vibrating bike for two hours. While I was doing that, the air was suddenly pierced by the loudest, shrillest scream I had ever heard, and I jumped about two feet off the ground.

It was my kid sister Bonita, who was only about seven or eight years old. She piled off the back steps and ran over to grab me around the waist. And she screamed again. *"Brother!"* she shrieked at the top of her voice. If you've ever heard Bonita scream, you can imagine what that did to my nervous system. I realized immediately that I did wrong when I, without thinking, reacted to the nerve-shattering scream by smacking my cute little kid sister, who only wanted to greet her beloved brother, right in the mouth. "SHUT! UP!" I yelled, and stood there shaking like a leaf, feeling like a heel for losing it like I did.

Okay, I know you're already on Bonita's side in this, so I'm sure you're going to enjoy what happened next. Bonita went running into the house, squalling. Mama came rushing out of the house, red faced. She had been washing dishes, and had a butcher knife in her right hand, dripping with sudsy water. She was on me in a flash, madder than a wet hen. I was six inches taller that she was, but it seemed at that moment that she was ten feet tall and towering over me. *"What did you do to that baby?"* she demanded, but didn't wait for an answer. I hollered when she slapped me along the tender ribs with the flat side of that butcher knife, and then the show was on. Bonita stood on the porch with a tear in her eye and a grin on her face and watched me dance while Mama gave me a thorough plow-cleaning whuppin' with the flat side of that big old butcher knife. I mean she made sure she smacked every inch of exposed flesh from belt to collarbone, front and back. I was hopping around like a neck-wrung chicken, hollering, "I'm sorry! I'm sorry!" I don't know how she kept from nicking me with the edge of the blade, but I was still a-bobbin' and a-throbbin' by the time she wore out and quit working me over.

Of course, Bonita was all right after I apologized. Not a mean bone in her body. Mama even grinned some after she cooled off, thinking of how funny I looked hopping around and around trying to get away. All was back to normal by suppertime, and I put away enough groceries to make the stinging feel better. But this story could have had a worse ending for me. You may not believe this, but I was grateful that Mama whipped me with that butcher knife, and here's why...

In her other hand, Mama was holding a skillet.

The Beloved Pastor of Pinson

The little farming community of Madie, in rural Lake County, Tennessee consisted mainly of a country store and a post office when John David Olhausen was born there on May 15, 1906. David grew up on a farm with three brothers and three sisters. Their parents were Walter and Naomi Neal Olhausen.

David was very young when he made his first commitment to the Lord, but he waited until he was eleven or twelve years old before he was ready to make a public profession of faith. It was during a Presbyterian revival, but he joined the local Methodist church the following Sunday.

There was never a time in his memory, David said, when he didn't want to be a preacher. Even as a small boy, whenever the little evangelist could round up a group of brothers and sisters and friends he would preach to them. Sometimes he would "get a testimony," as he put it, out of one of them, and

111

then they would all sing. He followed the model of pretty much every church service he'd ever been in.

When David was thirteen, his father died, and the hopeful young minister was forced to drop out of school at Ridgely, Tennessee to help work the family farm.

At the age of eighteen, David met and married a popular young lady from Gibson County by the name of Mary Bolerjack. With a twinkle in his eye, he would say he had to "beat out" a lot of competition to win her.

By the time their first three children were born, David's dreams of one day going to school to become a minister seemed out of the question. He was farming and working part time as a storekeeper just to keep his family clothed and fed, and this was during the Depression years. But the desire inside him would not go away, like a fire that would not be quenched. Finally, David promised God he would give up farming and storekeeping and surrender to preach, if the Lord would provide the means.

He went back and finished high school, studying right alongside his children. Learning of his commitment, friends would occasionally share a financial gift, just when it was needed most. Churches began asking David to preach for them, and would take love offerings. His own church also helped, and as God was faithful in providing finances in these ways, David also fulfilled his part of the bargain. He earned a degree from Lambuth College, and went on to get a seminary education by correspondence from Emory University.

David Olhausen was licensed to preach when he was 28. He never forgot any of the churches he served, and could name them all. He served four charges as a circuit preacher: Fowlkes, Martin, Pinson and Clopton. He pastored Grimes memorial in Memphis, Hays Avenue UMC in Jackson, Springdale in Memphis, and Bolivar First United Methodist Church. He was serving as pastor of Forest Heights UMC in Jackson when he retired in 1974.

"Retirement," however, was only a word to Brother Olhausen. He merely shifted into a new ministry of visiting the sick and shut-ins. The Jackson-Madison County General Hospital was on his weekly beat. He visited any patient he was told about, regardless of their faith or denomination, color, gender or age. He was so faithful in this ministry that there was even talk of naming a wing of the hospital after him.

After his official retirement, the Olhausens lived on the Davis Road in Pinson, and David returned to once again serve the churches where he had begun his ministry. He filled the pulpits at Pinson, Bear Creek, Montezuma, and Big Springs whenever the regular pastor was away. He also served as Visiting Pastor for Aldersgate UMC in Jackson during his retirement. David contracted bone cancer sometime in the 1980s, but it didn't stop his ministry. On his good days he continued to visit the sick and pray for them. He once stated, "I'll be a minister as long as I live."

And so he was. Though suffering bouts of excruciating back pain, he was still often seen in the pew, in his place on the

Lord's Day, giving his tithe and adding his fading voice to the praise of the one he served. In looking back over his life on one occasion, David said he saw little he would have done differently, unless he could have entered the ministry earlier. His hope for the Church was that the Holy Spirit would move and bring new life. His advice to us all was, "Have faith. Step out on it, and it will work."

David Olhausen died quietly in his sleep shortly before midnight on Saturday, March 25, 1989. A few minutes later, the clock heralded the beginning of a new day – Easter Sunday. Resurrection Day.

John David and Mary Bolerjack Olhausen had five children: James, Mary Ruth, Norma Jean, Joy, and Daris. This information is from an interview of David Olhausen by Joe McCormick in June 1988.

Redneck In Paris

Mission work is an adventure. In April 1995 it was my privilege to go to Africa to do some artwork on a series of health posters for a missionary in Bamako, Mali. Going and coming, I had to change planes in Paris, France. On the return trip my layover was long enough to allow for an afternoon of sightseeing. I would probably never get another chance to visit the Louvre. I had always dreamed of seeing Leonardo DaVinci's *Mona Lisa*.

Paris is a pretty good place to go take a look at if you want to see some old buildings. Downtown Paris is a jumble of really old buildings. And if you can read French you might find the graffiti along the Metro tracks interesting. Otherwise I'm not sure I could recommend Paris as a good place for a Tennessee hillbilly to go, at least not for relaxation.

I went there with all kinds of advice ringing in my ears, and it must have got me a little uptight. Nothing really worked out like I expected.

I thought I was going to see gendarmes on every corner directing traffic, and flocks of fashion models in designer clothes followed by herds of photographers. I thought there would be guys with big noses and pencil mustaches wearing turtleneck sweaters and berets, sitting at sidewalk cafes sipping wine and smoking cigarettes through long cigarette holders. I wanted to get me some pictures of lovers walking hand in hand beside the Seine, like in the movies. I was all set to fight my way through yapping packs of French poodles.

I didn't even see a dropping.

I did see a few couples sitting in the sun along the banks of the river, but to me they looked more like brain dead winos waiting out a hangover than lovers.

My education started at the airport. Charles de Gaulle Airport has two terminal buildings, an old one and a new one. Like airport terminals everywhere, neither one is a place you want to go to relieve stress.

I got off the plane at the old building, the one shaped like a guitar. Since I had a layover, I had to go through customs. That was so quick I had to blink. Did the guy ever look at my passport? I know he took the little declaration slip, because they had never given me one on the plane and the customs guy at the airport gave me one, which took about 15 seconds to fill out. Then I was through the line on my way downstairs to pick up my two suitcases (one full of my belongings and the other full to bursting with mail the missionaries in Africa had sent with me to put in the mailbox when I got back to the States). I had my baggage claim stub clutched in my sweaty hand and kept waiting for someone official looking to challenge me, so I could shove the stub in his face. But I just picked up my suitcases and walked right out on the street, with no one saying so much as aye, yes or no. I guess no one at the Paris Airport cares whose bags you walk out with. I took another look to make sure I had the right ones.

At a little desk I asked directions where to wait for a shuttle bus for my hotel, the Ibis. I went to the place they told me to wait. Thirty minutes later I hadn't seen any shuttle with the Ibis Hotel name on it. Finally, I happened to glance up, and noticed I was standing next to a phone with a sign in English over it that said you could use it to make reservations at the Ibis. I looked around guiltily to see if anyone was snickering. I picked up the handset and a female voice answered. I asked if they had a reservation for me. She checked and said no. *NO?* There I stood in the middle of Paris, France with no hotel reservation and fifty dollars in my pocket. Mentally I was thinking that there must be a canine branch to my travel agent's family tree, when the hotel clerk said, "At which hotel do you have the reservation?"

"You mean you got more than one?"

"Oh, yes, sir. Ibis has many hotels in France. There are three in Paris."

Trust them to pull something like that on me. Now I was really getting hot at my travel agent for omitting that little bit of information, but that's a hick travel agent for you. I guarantee you there wouldn't be more than one Ibis hotel in Paris, *Tennessee*.

The clerk asked me to look on my reservation sheet and give her the address, which I did. She told me which bus to catch. A few minutes later I saw one parking a few doors down, so I got on it and asked the driver if he would be passing by the address I had on the paper. He nodded and burnt rubber. I grabbed a handrail and tried to enjoy the ride, not at all sure the guy had understood my question. The anxiety of times like that eats me up. I didn't recognize anything, so I sure didn't know where I was going.

Finally, the bus skidded to a stop in front of the Ibis Hotel. I walked in and asked the clerk if he had a reservation for Joe McCormick. To my relief he said without hesitation, "Yes, I believe so." He checked me in, handed me a little plastic card key, and I started looking around for the guy who was supposed to be hovering around waiting to carry my bags up. I had a whole pocket full of one-dollar bills I was going to use to tip guys like him. After a minute I realized that this wasn't going to be like it is on TV, so I picked up my duct-taped suitcases and went on up to my room.

The room was nice. I wanted only to lie down on the double bed and sleep the day away. I had been up all day the day before, leaving Bamako at 11:45 at night. Sleeping on a plane might be possible if a person drank a lot, which I didn't. After 5 hours in the air and some time changes we landed at Charles de Gaulle (the pilot pronounced it Shah-de-Go) at 7:30A.M. I was wrinkled and red-eyed and really wasn't looking forward to any more stress. But I'd bragged around how when I got to Paris I was gonna go see me the Mona Lisa. So, I knew I had it to do.

I took a shower, changed my clothes and went down to the desk. I asked the clerk how to get to the Louvre and he told me it was very easy. Walk out the hotel door, catch the shuttle, get off at the Metro station, buy the Formula One ticket and ride all day on the subway, bus or train for one price. I thought I understood that the ticket would also admit me to museums around town, but as we shall see, something always happens between the transmitter and the receiver whenever someone is trying to give me instructions. Me, I'm a Sesame Street type of person. You got to repeat things to me over and over before I start to get it.

I got on the shuttle, clutching my camera bag. I called myself watching for something with a big "M" on it, for "Metro." I rode for thirty minutes, keeping a hawk eye on the signs. We passed intersections, crossed over, cut back, stopped at every airport terminal and suddenly the bus stopped back in front of my hotel. I was right back where I started from.

I got off and walked back inside. I collared that same clerk and said, "Did I miss something?"

He said, "Explain me, please."

Me being a paying customer, he didn't laugh but patiently went back over the instructions, which could not have been simpler. I got back on the shuttle thinking that maybe I had missed my calling by going into art. Probably my God-given purpose in life was to go around finding things that were simple to everyone else and screwing them up. I was sent here for that.

I never saw a big "M" but this time around I did read the sign on a big low building we stopped at. It was the train station, or Metro. The subway. The place where I was going to buy me a ticket that would make the rest of my day ridiculously simple.

I went up to a little window and asked for a Formula One ticket. The girl took my money (about $10.00) and shoved a big white envelope in my hands. Puzzled, I decided I'd better take a minute and think this through. What I held in my hand didn't look like a ticket, I don't care what formula they used. I picked me out a bench off in a corner away from everyone and sat down. I opened up the envelope, hoping there would be some kind of ticket inside. There was a big folding map of the city with the subway route marked. There was a plastic card about the size of a credit card and a little stiff paper stub. I think there was a letter explaining how to use all the stuff, but of course it was printed in French. I finally figured out that the little stub was what I really needed, but I stuck the plastic card in my shirt pocket, so it would be handy in case the police or somebody tried to arrest me for illegally riding a subway. I'm not dumb. When you wind up in somebody else's country you got to figure all the angles and be ready for surprises.

I sat there and watched until I saw somebody go through a turnstile, so I figured you had to do that to get to where the train was. But then some punk teenagers vaulted over the turnstiles, so that left me a mite uncertain as to the proper method of passing that barrier. Then I noticed a skinny girl holding a little stub in a slot on top of the turnstile machine. She yanked the little stub out and the turnstile bars turned as she went through.

So that's what you had to do. I fished the little ticket out of my pocket and walked up to a turnstile, looking real cool and casual, like I had been living in Paris all my life and going through a turnstile was just about the boringest thing a sophisticated world traveler like me could be called on to do. Holding my little cardboard ticket between thumb and forefinger I jabbed it down in the slot on top of the machine and started to step through the turnstile the way I'd seen the others do. I almost crippled myself when I walked into the bar. It didn't give. It stayed locked. I jabbed the ticket into the slot again and pushed. The bar stubbornly refused to move.

I tried again. *Jab, jab, jab, jab, jab!* Still nothing.

I tried another turnstile, with the same results. Exasperated, I backed off and set my shoulder bag on the floor and commenced to unzipping pockets, pretending I was looking for something (like maybe a bazooka to blow the gate off that dang turnstile, or a book of instructions on how to have a clue). What I was really doing was killing time while I scoped out the

121

situation. There had to be some way to get through that infernal gate.

Out of the corner of my eye I saw a guy walking fast come up to the turnstile, feed his ticket into a slot down on the *side* of the machine and *zip!* That little stub went through the guts of that machine quicker than castor oil and shot out the hole on top! The guy yanked his ticket stub out of the slot and pushed the turnstile bar out of his way, and off he went.

I looked within myself and didn't see anybody looking back.

But, once I see something done, I can do it, almost every time. As I approached the gate this time I had lost a little of my strut. Whether you know it or not, being stupid can take a lot of energy out of you. I regained some of my confidence, however, when lo and behold, the little stub worked when inserted into the proper little slot (I must say there were other places I would have liked to insert it, if only I could have found the guy who designed that blasted turnstile system). I proceeded down a flight of steps wondering vaguely if there had been some kind of lesson for me in the turnstile episode. But what the heck. Life is full of lessons that I never got. I applied the few brain cells I still had working to the problem of figuring out which train to get on.

French is a beautiful language, they say. Standing there beside the tracks trying to decipher the signs, I decided that the most beautiful language is the one you can read. I looked at my little guidebook and I looked at the signs, and they didn't match.

The different lines were color-coded. I still couldn't make any sense of it. I wasn't sure whether the blue line or the yellow line would take me to the Louvre. I looked through the open door of one of the trains and noticed that a map of the system was displayed up over the windows on the wall. I stepped in to have a closer look and suddenly the door behind me went, *"Ssssssssshp!"* like on Star Trek, and the train took off. I grabbed something to hold on to and looked around into the unsmiling faces of hard-eyed Parisians and mentally dared them to start something. Ready or not, I was on my way *somewhere* in Paris.

I took out the little subway guide and read some of the names of places I was supposed to pass on my way to the Louvre. Then I looked out the window to read the signs on the stations we stopped at. As you've already figured out, the names didn't match. I started to sweat. I recalled a song I once heard about a guy who kept going back and forth on the subway for years because he couldn't find the place where he was supposed to get off. I didn't want that.

Finally, I saw a sign coming up I thought I recognized. Frantically I thumbed through the guidebook and found that this place was indeed on my route. Immensely relieved, I found a seat and settled back trying to look bored like everybody else. I kept a thumb in the guidebook. If the next stop had the same name as the one in the book, I'd know I was headed in the right direction. I felt better, but I was still a bit uneasy. Up to now things hadn't been working out as slick as everybody had led me to believe they would. They had made it sound so simple that I half expected to see a sign light up over the door saying,

"LOUVRE - JOE, GET OFF HERE." Nothing I could read on that train said anything about the Louvre, but on my map I lined up where the Louvre was with a station that looked pretty close. Sure enough, that station came up next, and I almost knocked a fat lady down getting off. All I wanted now was to find an exit back out into the light of day. I needed me some air.

Now I've got to ask you to follow my line of reasoning pretty close, so you'll know that every step I took was entirely logical. I know you would have done the same thing I did. Simplest thing in the world, you get on a subway, you ride to your stop, you get off, climb the steps to the street and you're off for a delightful and fulfilling excursion on the exotic streets of gay Paree. I know you would have done exactly like me after you'd walked about a mile in that subway tunnel without finding any dang exit to the outside. You'd have turned yourself around and marched off along one of the other infernal offshoot tunnels that seemed to go on forever. Maybe you might not have mumbled the same words I did, but I predict you would have kept walking past little shops and snack joints, checking the signs at every intersection for something, anything you could make sense of. All I wanted was a simple little sign that said, "This way to daylight." In my world you got a right to expect that. We have things like that here to show us where to go and what not to touch or step in. No way I wouldn't have been able to fight my way out of a subway in the good ole U.S.A.

But I was in France. They did their signs in a different language, and for all I could tell they didn't give a hoot what you touched or what you stepped in or where you went. People were going in every direction. I decided to pick me out somebody to follow and see where they ended up. Surely these people went up for air sometime. I fell in behind a short bald guy with an umbrella, but he went through another turnstile and got back on another train. I was getting depressed.

I saw an information booth. Beverly always tells me I should ask directions, so I went over and asked a guy in a red coat how to get to the street. He smiled and pointed and told me how simple it was to go in that direction, turn left at something, turn right at something else, go through a turnstile and up the steps. I followed his directions and kept staying lost. As a matter of fact, I kept staying a little more lost than ever. I bobbed and weaved and ducked down every side tunnel I came to, but kept coming back to a big, brightly lighted intersection where people were crisscrossing like ants. I walked faster and faster, checking every possible avenue, only to keep running into dead ends or turnstiles leading to other trains, God forbid.

I wasn't mad at anybody anymore. I was scared.

To this day I can't tell you how I got out of that underground prison. All I remember is somehow I found myself entering a turnstile on the other side of which was a flight of steps leading upward. Thank you, God. I expected to see angels ascending and descending like Jacob's ladder.

Taking the steps two at a time I emerged into the blessed overcast of old downtown Paris. I hunted a bench and sat down to give my shoes time to quit smoking.

Looking around, I couldn't help being excited. Paris, France! *Man!* It was about like any other big city with traffic and all, and crowds of people stepping on each other except that here there were a lot more old, old buildings. Bronze statues here and there. Historic is what it was. I pulled out my city map and located the Louvre. Not over ten or fifteen blocks away by my reckoning. I was so glad to finally get out of that subway maze that I felt as happy as if I'd made a bullseye. To a man like me a town was no different than the woods. Those tall buildings over on the right were trees. Keep them on your right as you head up the street, and keep them on the left when you come back. I ran a thumb over my shoe soles to check the thickness remaining and struck out for the Louvre. Mona Lisa was waiting. Today in Paris I was going to see at least one smiling face.

The museum was big and old and U-shaped. I walked around it until I came to the inside of the U, a wide brick-paved courtyard with pigeons and sculpture all over the place and a glass pyramid right smack in the middle. As a matter of fact, there were some other smaller glass pyramids sticking up, too, and fountains spraying water everywhere. I headed for the big pyramid. That's where they said the tickets were bought for the museum. There were about 50 people in line outside the doors. It didn't take long to get inside and down some steps. Holy cow... was I back in another subway? I shivered at the thought. Some people were lined up at a ticket window, but I was still laboring under the belief that I had already bought all the ticket I needed to see all of Paris. I pulled out the Formula One card and crossed the lobby to another set of steps leading upward to the Italian art hall. A guard at the top stopped me, even though I flashed the Formula One card in her face. I suppressed my indignation when she told me that card did not allow me passage to this part of the Louvre. I stalked off to find a section where they had a guard who was a little more on top of things.

Another flight of steps, another hall, another guard. I flashed the card in her bored looking face and she almost let me past. Then she took another look at the card and waved me back. Exasperated, I weighed my chances of decking her and making a break for it down the hall. Looking at the babe's hatchet face, I reconsidered. She looked like she could take me.

"You mus' to go back and buy a ticket," she told me. Why couldn't they understand that I, a bonafide American tourist with camera bag and everything, had already *bought* a blooming ticket that was supposed to get me all over Paris and into every place but the mayor's private bathroom? At least I believed that was the kind of ticket I'd bought. I looked at the card. Hadn't somebody told me this thing was all I needed to see all of Paris?

"That card," the nice guard lady explained, "allows you to ride the Metro all day anywhere in Paris." She tried to hide her smile." But to see these exhibits you mus' go back downstairs and purchase a ticket."

Well, you don't need to hit me over the head with a brick. I went back down the steps and bought a ticket.

Finally (I couldn't believe it), I stood before the Mona Lisa. I gawked at the dingy looking little painting in the glass case and then looked around for the real one. Surely *that* wasn't the Mona Lisa, just hanging there on a nail like any other painting. Well, they had at least finally put it behind glass and roped off a little space in front, but there were no guards with machine guns standing there ready to cut you in two if you took a picture. People were doing that, too, with flash and everything. I pulled out my little borrowed camcorder and started videoing. The only thing I can say about the Mona Lisa is to quote Uncle Versey Ledbetter upon seeing the Gulf of Mexico for the first time: "I always thought it'd be bigger than that." The painting wasn't over a couple of feet tall.

As I left the building I saw why people had warned me to get there early. The plaza was filled with people waiting to get in. The line stretched out of sight around the end of the building. If they had been there when I arrived I would never have seen the Mona Lisa.

The sky was overcast and threatening rain, and the air was nippy as I walked along the Quay beside the River Seine. All my life I'd seen paintings of this place. Over on the other side was where the artists of old had set up a colony. They called that the "Left Bank." Matisse, Van Gogh, Cezanne and all the other French impressionists used to hang out over there. If their first impression of Paris was like mine, I could see why their paintings always looked blurred.

I walked out on a bridge called Pont Neuf, which means "New Bridge." The guidebook said that nowadays it's the oldest bridge in Paris. I took some pictures of the island called Isle de la Cité, pointed at the end like the nose of a ship. I wished I had time to go out on it and see Notre Dame Cathedral. Just out of curiosity, I wanted to check the sidewalk in front of the cathedral to see if I could spot any stains remaining from where the hunchback took his dive.

I checked my watch. I was tired when I started out on this caper, and now I was about wasted. All I wanted was to just get back to the hotel and crash. I left the bridge and started walking back down toward the subway station. All at once a woman dressed like a bag lady and a ragged little girl who looked to be about ten years old swooped in from nowhere and surrounded me. They both had one hand stuck out palm up and with the other hand they were frisking me, jabbering away in a language that didn't sound like French to me. They slapped every pocket I had and touched every zipper on my camera bag before I knew what was going on. Suddenly I knew I'd had it. These were gypsies and they were going to steal me blind. I could already hear my mama back home telling the story to her friends: "Well, I been warning the boy about running off on them trips. I told him he was plump enough they'd eat him in Africa. Never counted on the gypsies gettin' to him first. Picked him clean, them gypsy women did. Wandered three days out of his head before the cops caught him, wearing nothing but a T-shirt, wavin' some kinda little ticket stub, trying to force his way into that there Loove place."

They patted me down pretty thorough. Embarrassed, I was slapping at their hands going, "No-No! No tengo dinero!" Then I remembered they don't speak Spanish in Paris, so I tried

129

French: "No gottee monee," I spluttered, grabbing frantically at every place I felt fingers touch. This was getting serious.

The mother and daughter looked at one another when they heard me switch languages. Then they started jabbering again in another language that wasn't the one they'd used before, and it wasn't French either. Then they redoubled their efforts, and if it hadn't been me they were working over I might have admired their teamwork. With my left hand locked in a death grip on my camera bag, I only had one hand for defense. They stayed one step ahead of me. By the time I'd reach up to slap a hand away from my shirt pocket I'd feel another hand on my billfold pocket. I've always joked about the one-armed paperhanger with the seven-year itch, and now I know how it feels.

Right about then I was fixing to get myself into a pretty good panic. Those gypsies were going to have me for lunch. But suddenly my natural country boy cunning kicked in. Where I grew up not everybody made moonshine, but everybody shared the same attitude about the po-lice. Let the high sheriff come cruising up and down the roads and folks started looking for the nearest escape route, whether they were guilty or not. Just about the time I was ready to admit they had me, it came to me to nod my head toward the street and point. It worked. They thought I was warning them that a cop was coming over to check them out. Like a flash they were lost in the crowd and I beat it in the other direction.

I found me a bench away from the crowd and sat down to take inventory. I was sure I was going to be shy a billfold at least. But to my utter relief I found nothing missing. Except for maybe a few nerve endings. God is so good to hayseeds.

That's it for me, I said to myself. I can take a hint. I hauled my stuff off that bench and started looking for that hole that would take me back down into the subway. I didn't like the idea much of getting caught in that rat maze again, but I had this Formula One ticket, and by golly if they wouldn't let me use it in that art museum I was for sure going to get my money's worth riding that underground train. At least now I was a hardened veteran. I'd figure out some way to get back out into the fresh air once I got to the end of the line.

There's not a whole lot of other stuff to say about my trip to Paris. I didn't look right nor left out of that subway train window on the way back. I had seen as much of the elephant as I was interested in. I made it back to my hotel and breathed a sigh of relief once the door closed behind me. I went up to my room and hunkered down to watch TV until suppertime. I ate in the hotel dining room, but I didn't take any chances. I ordered a hamburger. Next morning, I caught the shuttle back to the airport and was deliriously happy to find that they hadn't lost my reservation on the plane or something. I buckled myself down in that nice soft seat and tightened the belt extra snug. I wanted to feel secure. I needed to feel secure. For the whole eight-hour flight I didn't even get up to go to the bathroom.

Aw, I guess Paris was all right, if you like to see old buildings and hear people talk funny. But for an experienced and sophisticated world traveler like me it really wasn't all that much. Overrated, really. They didn't even know what I was talking about when I ordered *French* fries with that hamburger.

(ALMOST) BIBLICAL

Ahazia and Elijah
II Kings 1

Yellow - gray dust, kicked up by the prancing feet of the nervous teams, billowed out from around the heavy chariot wheels, swirling up to settle as fine powder on the blue military cloak of the stern figure holding the reins. Mentally Captain Balizar cursed the dust and the insufferable Samarian heat, and everything else about this stupid fool's errand. *Fifty men* to go out and fetch one old prophet and bring him to the king? Ridiculous!

Balizar glanced back over his shoulder at the hard faced men marching behind him. He hadn't thought it necessary to issue full battle armor for this type of mission. The heat was bad enough as it was. Since there would be no opposing force to worry about, he saw no need to burden the men down with all that weighty protective gear. Each man shouldered a heavy spear and wore a sheathed sword. That would be more than enough. Balizar squinted through the dust at a hulking figure slogging along at the head of the column, and a cynical smile quirked his lips. Sergeant Jakobbi was a one-man army himself. Almost seven feet tall and built like an ox, the sergeant had once killed six men with his bare hands in a drunken brawl. The six men had all been armed. The feat had made Jakobbi a famous man. His ruthlessness and cruelty were legendary, and he was feared by all.

Sergeant Jakobi would have been enough. No need for the whole contingent to be out here in these dry, godforsaken hills hunting for one old man. Everyone else could have been kicked back in their bunks at the barracks, or sharing a cool bottle of wine with a maid. The captain mopped his brow with the sleeve of his tunic. Even standing watch at the palace would be better than marching out here in this heat, eating half the dust in Samaria. Balizar tightened his jaw, feeling fine grit between his teeth. He swore softly. Jakobbi would have been enough.

But Balizar was too disciplined to let his thoughts show on his face. The decision had not been his. When the king told you to do something, you did it. You didn't stand around arguing, no matter how stupid the orders sounded. That was no way to advance in this man's army. Rather, knowing Ahaziah's temper, it would be the best way he knew to get a sudden discharge the hard way - by sword point.

The king wanted fifty men, the king got fifty men. End of argument.

Why had the old fool let himself get so messed up anyway, for Baal's sake, walking through an upper floor lattice partition like a two-year-old kid, for crying out loud. It was a wonder the king had lived this long, with that piece of lattice sticking out of his fat paunch.

Balizar clucked the team to a slightly faster pace, hoping to pull ahead of his own dust. King Ahaziah, in his own discretely guarded opinion, was a first class idiot in the first place for walking through a wall like some kind of a clown, and in the second place for sending someone to ask the gods if he was going to get well. As if the gods knew, or cared.

The whole question of gods meant little to Balizar. He paid lip service to whatever god or deity happened to be in vogue, but he trusted in nothing but his own strong right arm and a sharp sword. And, of course, money. It had been his experience that either money or a sword could get you just about anything you wanted.

The king was pretty superstitious, though. He burned a lot of valuable incense to Baal, a god of the pagans in these parts. They had worshipped Baal for centuries, but he'd never seen where it did them any good. When the government changed hands it was usually because somebody with more chariots and swords came along and took over, and Baal didn't seem to be around helping out much during such times.

The best he could understand it, Baal was not so much a god anyway, as some divine, all-pervading power, or principle of the universe. Balizar wasn't one to probe too deeply into the finer points of religion. He showed up at the temple and dropped a few coins into the moneybox because it was expected of him, but as far as he was concerned it was all hogwash. Of course he'd never let the king hear him say that.

The captain removed his hard leather helmet and wiped his forehead with a corner of his robe. He put a blunt thumb up against one nostril and blew forcefully, ejecting a wad of clotted dust. He repeated the process with the other nostril. Settling his helmet back on his head, Balizar laughed cynically. What a bunch of chickenhearted ambassadors the king had sent to see if they could find an oracle to give them a word from Baal. So, while on their way to fulfill that errand, they meet some wild-eyed hick standing in the middle of the road, blocking their way. He sends them packing back to the king with a message from the "real" God. As Balizar heard it, this wild man says to the king's ambassadors, "Is it because there is not a God in Israel that you go to inquire of Baal-zebub?" And then this wild man was supposed to have said to them that they should tell the king that he was dead meat. What a story.

Balizar frowned. In spite of himself he had to admit, it was pretty dramatic. Something about the message, maybe its audacity, or the way it was phrased, gave it the ring of truth. Maybe this old prophet they met - Elijah they had called him - maybe he was just a convincing speaker. The king's delegation had certainly been impressed enough to turn right around without argument and go fogging it back to the king with the message. And now Ahaziah wanted the old coot hauled in.

So Balizar, captain of his fifty, came full circle in his thinking. And at that moment his thoughts were interrupted by a cry from somewhere ahead. He quickly brought his chariot to a halt by a pull on the reins. Staring intently through the heat waves in front of him, he saw his advance scout materialize and come on at a steady trot. Halting beside the captain's chariot, the sweating scout saluted, taking a moment to catch his breath. The heat was suffocating.

"I found him, sir," the scout reported, pointing toward a low, rocky hill just ahead. "If you look right up there at the top, a little to the left of center, you can see him. He's just sitting there." The scout shrugged his shoulders. "He's not saying a word. Hasn't moved a muscle. Just sitting there staring out into space."

Balizar put both hands up to his forehead, bracketing his eyes to shield them from the sun, and squinted through the veils of heat. At this distance he could barely make out the dark shape, definitely a man, sitting squarely in the heat of the midday sun. He wasn't moving. Must be crazy or dead, Balizar thought, turning to order his men forward. "Let's get this over with," he growled to no one in particular. He popped the reins on the sweaty rumps of the horses, lifting them into a tired trot.

The column halted at the foot of the hill. Balizar leaned a hairy elbow on the rail of his chariot and shifted his sword belt where it was beginning to chafe his hip.

"Hey! Old man!" he yelled at the solitary figure brooding at the top of the hill. "Get down here, *now!* You're going to see the king." The hill wasn't all that high, but Balizar saw no need for him or any of his men to exert themselves by climbing up there to fetch the crazy old man.

"Man of God," Balizar mocked, "get your scrawny carcass down here!" He looked at sergeant Jakobi and winked. Jakobi grinned evilly. Where cruelty was concerned both men were cut from the same pattern.

"You hear me, old man?" the captain yelled, taunting. "You're going to get to see the king himself. You're going to be somebody!" He lowered his voice and said aside for Jakobi's ears, "Somebody dead." The calloused sergeant threw back his head and laughed out loud, showing broken yellow teeth behind his wide, sun-cracked lips.

The man on top of the hill stirred. He had sat as if he were deaf, leaning forward with his legs outspread, elbows propped on his knees, staring into space. He wasn't a particularly old man, but his ragged and unkempt apparel and emaciated body made him appear ancient. A thick beard and long, unruly hair almost obscured the face, which never even turned toward the soldiers, but continued to stare impassively out over the desert. Only a large beak of a nose broke the shaggy profile. The man's thin body was as hairy as his face. He was clothed in worn and soiled leather. A filthy robe woven from some kind of animal hair lay wadded up beside him on his rocky perch. Altogether the man was a pretty sorry specimen of humanity. Looking at him, Balizar, who was skeptical at best of the existence of any God, was even more convinced now.

"Jakobi," he chuckled, "take a look at that, would you?" He pointed up the hill at the prophet. "Ask yourself this question: If you were an almighty God, would you pick a miserable hairball like that to be your mouthpiece?" Both men collapsed against the side of the captain's chariot, laughing uproariously.

The man at the top of the hill waited until the laughter of the soldiers had subsided. Then he spoke. He didn't bother to look at them. He spoke in a normal voice, so that they had to strain to hear him.

"If I be a man of God," he said, gazing wearily across the barren landscape, "if I be a man of God, let fire come down from heaven... and consume you..."

The shaggy head turned finally, and even at this distance Balizar felt the shock of that stare. He felt the insolence drain out of him as he looked across the heat waves into eyes like coals of fire. He saw the beard wag as the lips moved, and he heard the next words distinctly. It was the last thing he ever heard on earth:

"...and your fifty."

Balizar's tongue clove to the roof of his mouth as he saw the flame descending out of the sky. The great whirling column of fire hurtled down at them with incredible speed. There was no chance to avoid it. In the final millisecond of his life, the arrogant, unbelieving captain had time only for a shocking realization that there was indeed a God, and his name wasn't Baalzebub. *Oh, why hadn't he seen...*

And then there was no more time. There was only a swift, roaring, all-consuming hell for Ahaziah's captain and his fifty.

...

For hours, Othiel the shepherd lad had waited, until his hiding place was no longer in the shade. The sun was beginning to burn the back of his neck and the sand was hot under his knees. But the boy feared to move from the place where he knelt to seek the shadow of the overhanging rocks. He had seen what happened to the soldiers when they taunted the man of God. As long as he held himself still and made no noise perhaps he would not attract the same fate.

Despite the heat the lad shivered. He had not fully recovered from the shock of seeing a bolt of fire suddenly split the sky wide open and shoot down to consume an entire troop of foot soldiers. He looked at the place where the soldiers had stood. There was absolutely nothing left but a broad scorched area on the plain, with the footprints of fifty men and wheel marks of a horse-drawn chariot leading up to it. Not a brass buckle, not a sword, not a rivet from the carriage remained. Little flecks of sunlight glinted off globules of glass that formed from the superheated sand.

At the top of the rocky hill, the man of God continued his vigil - unmoving, unperturbed, his brooding gaze bent over the smoky desert. Nervously the lad watched him, darting his eyes from the prophet on the hilltop to the small flock of sheep in the valley below. The boy had climbed to an elevated vantage point on the hillside so he could watch his flock as they fed beside the trickling stream below. He never expected to witness such a spectacle as he had just beheld.

Another uncomfortable hour passed. The sheep grazed contentedly beside the stream, a few of them resting in the shade of some low - growing brush. The young shepherd was trying to summon enough courage to slip down the hill and drive his flock away from the place, when he heard a noise in the distance that drew his attention. He peeped around the corner of his covert and cold chills ran up and down his spine. There from the direction of the city, following the footsteps of the first troop, marched another band of fifty!

Instinctively the boy ducked, and while the prophet's eyes were watching the soldiers, the boy darted quickly into the shaded portion of a nest of boulders. Should another bolt of fire come from the sky, he wanted all the cover he could find.

Captain Akkub ordered his tanned young driver to draw rein, bringing his lathered team to a halt at the edge of a curious circle of blackened ground. Akkub called for a water bottle. Taking the water skin from a subordinate, the overweight, effeminate looking officer raised it high and squirted tepid water over his hot face and into his corpulent mouth. He rinsed his mouth and spat, then drank. Tossing the water skin back to its owner, the captain looked around. Hands on hips, he calmly assessed the situation with a critical eye. He saw no enemy. His wary eye had caught the movements of the shepherd boy, and had dismissed him as no threat. His scouts had circled the hill, finding no enemy lying in wait. Only one dark figure sat at the summit, unmoving, staring stonily out over the desert. He seemed to pay no attention to the band of armed warriors gathered below.

Akkub fingered his sword. Insolent old fool, he thought. Who does he think he is, ignoring a summons from the king? Sitting there dressed in his rotten rags, looking like a filthy beggar, thumbing his nose at the royal guard. Akkub sniffed. It was going to be a pleasure watching one of his muscular soldiers drag the mangy scarecrow down the hill by the matted hair of his head. Man of God indeed! What kind of hillbilly god would a ragged old beggar like that represent? Preposterous!

Akkub felt a stir of pride in the superiority of his own religion. Actually, the cynical captain was much like the first captain, in that he had long since decided that, from what he had seen of the seamy side of life, belief in some kind of divine being was for fools, although he had never voiced this to anyone. He had never trusted anyone in this world, let alone some other-worldly deity that you couldn't even see. Oh, he didn't mind if others believed in all the mumbo - jumbo. He supposed that religion was as good a sedative as any for superstitious minds. As for himself, he would depend on his wits, a well-tempered sword, and perhaps a bag of gold wouldn't hurt. He always strove to maintain a slight advantage over his enemy, which was one of the reasons he had risen to his position as a captain in the king's royal guards. In spite of his apparent softness, Akkub was totally ruthless. He felt perfectly capable of handling his own destiny. When it came right down to it, he worshipped nothing or nobody so much as himself, and it would have flattered him to be told that he was his own god. As for religion, if he must profess one or the other, he vastly preferred the company of one of the state religion's prostitutes or temple eunuchs to the harsh loneliness dealt to this old prophet by his God.

Oh, well - enough daydreaming. It was time to attend to the matter at hand. Akkub was still puzzled about why the first of the king's troops had failed to bring the old buzzard in. Sometimes the life was hard, unless one could find certain amusements to pass the time, as did Akkub, but surely they wouldn't have all deserted en masse? What was more likely was that they perhaps encountered a rum wagon on the road, and the whole bunch were probably lying drunk in some oasis. For whatever reason, none of that first fifty or their captain had returned to the palace with the old prophet. One would think there would have been some report of their whereabouts. It seemed they had simply dropped off the earth.

Be that as it may, the king had finally gotten tired of waiting and sent Akkub out with his men.

His body gone slightly soft from the dissolute life he led, Akkub was nevertheless valued by the king for his dispassionate cruelty. He was very efficient in dealing with the dirty jobs that others might be too squeamish to carry off successfully. Akkub killed easily, with no conscience. He liked killing because it helped him think of himself as a brave man, when in reality he was the greatest of cowards. His vanity and pride required daily reinforcement. To retain his self-image of superiority, it was necessary for him to continually be proving himself. He had become an insatiable predator with a pathological need for victories. The men he had around him were all hand-picked because of their similar blood lust.

Swearing under his breath, the impatient captain saw that there would be no opportunity for glory in this detail. There would be no pitched battles against superior odds, no chance of promotion. Just another desert hike for the troops to grumble about. Might as well get it over with.

Leaning lazily against one side of his chariot, Akkub propped a foot on the opposite rail. Cupping his hands around his mouth he whistled shrilly, startling the horses. Trace chains rattled and the whistle echoed across the hill. The old prophet sitting up there on the rock turned a weary eye toward the sound.

"Hey, old man!" Akkub called irritably, "get your skinny bones down here, now! You're late for your appointment with the king." For some reason his voice seemed unusually loud. The air was hot and still. One of the horses stamped a hind foot and swished his tail at a horsefly. There were no other sounds in the charged atmosphere.

Akkub suddenly felt a prickling sensation on the back of his neck. His hair bristled. Alarmed, he took a quick look around, but saw nothing suspicious. His fifty troopers stood in proper formation but with bored expressions. A simple guard detail with no reason to maintain battle alertness.

But that old man up there seemed just a bit too unimpressed, too confident. The sight of fifty armed men should have worried him a little more than he appeared to be.

The captain looked around again. He barked an order for the men to look alert, half expecting to see an armed force materialize from the rocky hillside, but there was no one. Only the top of a little shepherd boy's head peeping over a boulder.

Enough hesitation! Akkub straightened his slack posture and once more cupped his hands around his mouth. This time he literally bellowed. "Hey, you - man of God... *I said get down here - RIGHT NOW!*"

Echoes of his voice rolled away in the hot stillness. The man of God swatted at a fly and scratched under an armpit. When he spoke his voice was scarcely loud enough to carry, but the shepherd boy in his rocky covert heard every word distinctly.

"If I be a man of God," the prophet said, "let fire come down from heaven and consume you and your fifty."

"Lord, spare me!" The shepherd lad cried, as he saw for the second time that day the blinding flash which left him momentarily without vision. He stood frozen in place until he could see again, and then what he saw, or didn't see, brought a frightened whimper from his throat. Once more the plain was swept clean. There was no trace of the band of soldiers. Only another blackened circle upon the sands. A thin wisp of black smoke rose lazily into the still air.

The simple lad could take no more. His trembling legs received sudden strength and he fled in terror down the hillside. Throwing stones and beating at his surprised flock with a stick, he rounded up the sheep and drove them in a wide circle around the shoulder of the hill and back toward the city. Even in his haste, however, he was careful to keep to ravines that would hide him from the prophet of God, and to avoid the awful black circles of death.

...

The hour was late. Captain Zadditha and his hastily assembled troops emerged from the western gate into the amber glare of the descending sun. Night would fall before they returned from their mission, but the matter was urgent. The king's temper was near the boiling point. Twice already he had sent officers out with their escorts to bring a man in from the hills. Neither band had returned, and the king's patience was stretched to the limit. He was not accustomed to waiting for a subject of the realm to answer a royal summons. Zadditha knew that if this third sortie failed to produce results there would be serious consequences to pay. The king was grievously injured and in a venomous mood. He would not be in a state of mind to look with favor on the next captain of fifty who failed him. Zadditha swallowed his apprehension. He had no idea what had become of the first two contingents, but if they - all battle-hardened and hand-picked warriors - had been unable to carry out their orders, Zadditha knew that the possibilities of his success were bleak.

An honest, straightforward man in his mid-forties, the still vigorous and youthful looking captain had no ambitions for glory in battle, though he was capable enough. He fought, and fought well when called upon. But he much preferred diplomacy. War was so costly in terms of materials and men. In his view, head-to-head conflict was to be avoided whenever possible. However, when diplomacy failed, he did not hesitate to fight, and he fought to win.

This time, however...well...he just didn't know. Something or someone had prevented the other two groups from returning to post with their prisoner in hand. Zadditha had taken precautionary measures, equipping his men with extra armament and armor. Before they marched he had called the soldiers to attention and made a short, but effective speech to bring them to a state of mental preparedness to meet whatever they might have to face. They marched out of the city as alert and battle-ready as any troop he had ever commanded.

A flock of swiftly moving sheep swept around a bend in the road, blocking the path of the soldiers. The captain brought his team to a halt, waiting impatiently for the flock to pass. A small shepherd boy appeared from the cloud of dust following the sheep. He waved his arms frantically, trying to attract the captain's attention. He ran around the straggling line and approached the chariot breathlessly. "Oh, Excellency," he stammered, throwing himself face down on the ground at the horses' feet, "you must stop! You must not go to that place!"

"Boy, what is the matter with you?" Zadditha demanded. "What has happened?"

The lad picked himself up off the ground and raised a tear-streaked grimy face to the officer. "It was horrible there, sir," he sobbed. "Fire came down from the sky and burned up all the soldiers."

"What in the world are you talking about, boy?" Zadditha handed his reins to one of the soldiers and stepped down from the chariot. Placing both hands on the lad's shoulders, he looked sternly into the upturned face, which was pale, despite a smeared layer of dust. The thin shoulders trembled under the captain's hands.

In a gentler tone the captain asked again, "What is it, son? Tell me...what have you seen?"

Othiel drew a deep, shuddering breath and let it out in a long sigh. The strong hands of the captain on his shoulders helped to steady him. He collected his thoughts and began to tell about the fire that fell from the sky.

"I - I took my sheep to the regular place to water them and...and then I went up on the hill a little way to watch them from there. I didn't see the man of God until I heard the soldiers coming." The lad had calmed somewhat, but the fear had not left his eyes. He wiped a hand across his face, smearing the dust even more.

"When I stood up to look, there was captain Balizar with a troop of men standing at the foot of the hill, calling for the man of God. Then I saw him, sitting at the top of the hill. He wasn't doing anything. He didn't try to run or get away. He..." At this point the child's voice broke and tears appeared in his eyes. "He only said some words, which I barely heard, and then..."

"Then what, boy? Go ahead - spit it out."

"Sir, I'm afraid you will think I'm lying."

"Just tell me what you saw. I'll decide what I think about it."

"I...I saw a blazing sheet of fire come down from the heavens, and Balizar and his men were burnt up!" The lad blurted it out and stood waiting for the captain to laugh.

But Zadditha didn't laugh. He felt a cold chill go down his spine. He had a premonition about this man he was supposed to arrest. There were a lot of men in Israel who liked to strut around drawing attention to themselves by their self-styled prophetic utterances. This man wasn't one of those. Zadditha's thoughts underwent a rapid readjustment as he reappraised the situation.

The boy continued: "I was still there when the second captain came with his fifty. I was afraid to move."

Seeing the fear that haunted the boy's eyes, Zadditha could imagine the terror he must have felt. It would have been quite a traumatic experience for a child his age to watch men being burned alive.

"I was hiding for a long time before the second band of soldiers came. It got hot in the sun, but I was afraid the man at the top of the hill would see me if I tried to move into the shade. He - he was *scary*." The boy licked his lips. He used his hands nervously in describing the scene. Zadditha kept quiet and let him talk.

"The next men who came were burnt up too, captain. You must stay away from there or the same thing will happen to you."

Zadditha had already been thinking about that. He sent the shepherd lad on his way and pondered his situation. If the boy was telling the truth, this wasn't going to be as simple as it looked on the surface. The captain was certain of two things: The boy had seen *something* that had frightened him half to death, and *something* had happened to prevent the other two bands of fifty from returning to the king. Zadditha didn't like the way things were shaping up. He didn't like it at all. He had no desire to end up as a burnt offering for Elijah's God.

He gave some thought to that. In his experience he had seen a lot of religious activity, most of which he regarded as pure theatrics. Pompous holy men controlling men's lives with their magic and intimidation. To maintain the proper level of fear, the rituals usually involved bloodletting, and sometimes the blood was human. On those occasions, he had noticed, death always came at the hands of some priest or shaman. Never had any of the gods been known to do the job themselves.

Perhaps...perhaps there really was a God. Perhaps the one Elijah served was the *real* God. Zadditha suddenly felt strangely cold.

He knew he couldn't stand there undecided forever. His men were looking at him. He couldn't let them see the doubt that troubled his soul. He had to go ahead. There really was no way out of it. He had his orders, and Zadditha was too well disciplined to disobey an order. He sighed, and waved the column forward. His team leaned into their traces. He gripped the side rail of his chariot and applied his thoughts to the task ahead. The sweat running down the center of his back underneath his tunic was not altogether caused by the westering sun.

...

The prophet had not moved from his place. Zadditha, captain of the third fifty, realized that he had secretly been hoping that by the time he and his soldiers arrived at the site, their quarry would have long since made himself scarce. Bearing the king's wrath for returning empty handed could certainly be no worse than facing a flame from heaven.

Zadditha grinned sheepishly at himself. Did he really believe what the shepherd boy had said about the fire coming down to consume a hundred men and their captains? He looked down at the scorched rocks and sand around the area where he had halted his chariot, and decided he believed. A chill went down his spine. He believed every word. Was he destined to mingle his own ashes with those of his comrades in arms here on this barren plain?

Tentatively he stepped down from the chariot and handed the reins to a soldier. His knees felt weak, and he wondered if his courage was going to fail him in this strange situation. Zadditha had no trouble admitting to himself when he was scared, and this was one of those times. It was that very quality that defined the faithful captain as a truly courageous man, for he never let his fear stop him from doing his duty.

There was something here beyond the ken of the human mind. Intuitively Zadditha sensed the presence of an unseen power, against which swords and spears and human courage were nothing. He removed his helmet in an unconscious act of reverence. He had no idea how his predecessors had handled the situation, but he was going to treat the man sitting so quietly up on the hill with respect. With his heart in his throat, half expecting a tongue of flame to strike him at every step, he began to climb the hill.

Elijah watched the third emissary of the king climb slowly up the hill. The prophet was not as calm as he seemed, though it was not fear of the king's army that moved him. He had walked with the Lord Jehovah for many years and had seen him do wonderful and impossible things. But he never got used to it. The raw power of Almighty God was a frightful thing to behold. It was unsettling. Elijah shuddered at the memory of the 450 prophets of Baal at Mount Carmel. Every one slain as a sign to Israel. And that time Elijah had put his own hand to the sword. It was a time of drastic measures, all to prove to the people whom God had chosen that there was still a God in Israel, and he wasn't this impotent god of fertility they lusted to follow. At that time also God had sent fire down from heaven, consuming not only the bullock Elijah had laid upon the altar, but also the

154

very stones of the altar itself, and the water that had been poured over it all. Elijah shook his shaggy head. He still found it hard to believe. God didn't take it lightly when seducing spirits tried to lead his people astray.

But at Mount Carmel their hearts had been only temporarily turned. Now here was another king sending messengers to inquire of Baal, willfully ignoring the painful lessons of the past. Elijah sighed wearily. Would they never learn? He was getting so tired of crying out to a people who didn't want to hear about a God they must obey. Baal was much easier on them. His priests taught that he could be appeased with a few blood sacrifices, and his rituals appealed greatly to the sensual nature of unregenerate man. Elijah suddenly felt so inadequate. He was one man against the sin nature of man running rampant. He remembered a time when God had assured him that he was not the only man standing against the tide, but sometimes, when he saw how eager the people were to turn their backs on the Lord, he had to wonder.

And now the fire was coming again. Would it do any good, or would this, too, be soon forgotten? Elijah looked with pity upon the middle-aged captain laboring up the hill, expecting to see another example of God's wrath burning away at the rebellion of Israel.

But something was different about this man. Elijah felt a check in his spirit. He sensed his inward hearing grow attentive to the voice of God.

Zadditha fell to his knees before Elijah. He dropped his helmet in the rocky soil beside him. The prophet noticed that the man wore no sword. In his attitude there was none of the arrogance of the first two captains. This veteran soldier, vested with authority of the king and backed up by the might of the royal army, was now sincerely humbling himself before the prophet of God. At least he knew enough to fear for his life and show respect for a messenger of the Almighty. Elijah felt no harshness rising in his spirit for this man.

"Oh man of God," the captain said hesitantly, keeping his head lowered reverently, "I beg you...let my life be precious in your sight, and let the lives of these fifty, your servants..." he stretched a trembling hand toward his puzzled troops. "Let their lives be precious in your sight." Elijah drew in a deep breath, and the captain looked up quickly, continuing on before the prophet had a chance to speak.

"I heard how the fire came down from heaven and consumed the two captains of the former fifties with their fifties: Therefore I simply ask you to let our lives be as precious to you and your God as they are to us."

Outwardly Elijah remained as stone faced as before, but inwardly he was listening to the voice of God. For the space of several heartbeats he didn't know what he was supposed to do. This man had not come to shake his fist in God's face, as had the others. Elijah found himself hoping that the man might receive better treatment than his predecessors, though he admitted to himself that they had only gotten what they deserved. He had no sympathy for the strutting little tyrants who thought they were big enough to thumb their noses at the eternal God with impunity. Or at his prophets, for that matter. Elijah was happy to see that God had agreed with him on that point.

When the angel spoke it startled the prophet so much that he jumped reflexively. Why did they always have to *do* that? Right in the ear, without warning. Doing business with God certainly didn't do much for a prophet's nerves.

"Go down with this man," the voice of the angel said. "Be not afraid of him."

Elijah waited a moment while his heartbeat returned to normal. As there was nothing more forthcoming from the angel, Elijah rose stiffly from his seat on the rock. By the look on the man's white face, he guessed that the captain must have also seen the angel standing behind him. Chuckling sympathetically, he bent and gathered up his rough goat hair mantle. Tossing it over his shoulder he stretched, trying to relieve the stiffness that had settled in his body during his day - long vigil on top of the mountain. "All right," he said, beckoning for the captain to lead off. "Let's go see the king."

...

"Elijah! I knew it! I knew it had to be you," king Ahaziah rasped weakly, glaring at the hairy, roughly dressed figure standing over his bed. Flushed with fever, the king's bloated face was greasy with sweat. The pain in his side caused his breath to come in ragged gasps. He was already too weak to sit up in bed, but the hatred radiating from his burning eyes was as strong as ever. Elijah had never understood why the man obstinately refused to listen to anything having to do with the God of Israel, the only God who could do anything for anybody. Ahaziah insisted on bowing his knee to a filthy imitation of the real God, the only God there was, really. Elijah shook his head sadly. As rulers of a people, kings were supposed to be a cut above in the brain department, but if Ahaziah were any example, kings could be as stupid as anybody else.

"Now that I've finally got you here, I demand some answers from you, Elijah." The king's breathing was labored, but he seemed to draw strength from his anger at the prophet.

"Why didn't you come when I first summoned you?" Suspicion crossed his face. "And what do you know about the whereabouts of two bands of soldiers I sent out to fetch you? What sort of trickery...?"

"Ahaziah," Elijah interrupted, "will you never understand? Will you remain in rebellion until the end?" The sick man's face turned a deeper red, and a strangled retort rose in his throat, but Elijah continued: "Is it because there is no God in Israel that you send to inquire of Baal? Are you really stupid enough to believe you'd get an answer from a dumb idol? You think a piece of *stone* knows whether you're going to live or die?" He shook his head in disgust.

Elijah massaged the back of his neck through the tangled mass of his hair. "Well, here is God's word to you Ahaziah..." The king's bitter retort died in his throat. The words of the prophet congealed in the air, having a power of their own.

"Thus sayeth the LORD..."

In his bones Ahaziah knew that the *real* God, the Almighty, maker of heaven and earth, the God of Abraham, Isaac, and Jacob was about to speak. Everyone in the room held their breath.

"Thus sayeth the LORD, forasmuch as you have sent messengers to inquire of Beelzebub the god of Ekron, is it because there is no God in Israel to inquire of his word? Therefore, you shall not come down off that bed on which you are gone up."

The king's face had turned a chalky white. He stared in horror at Elijah out of hollow eyes, wishing he could scoff in disbelief at the words he was hearing. But he knew in his sinking heart that he was indeed receiving his verdict from the living God.

"You shall not come down off that bed, but you shall surely die!"

Ahaziah dropped like a limp rag back onto his bed as the prophet turned and stalked from the room. No one lifted a hand against Elijah. Then he was gone, and along with him the presence of God. In a room crowded with people; wife, family members, attending physicians and a host of servants, Ahaziah stared blankly at the ceiling, alone with the knowledge that he was as good as dead. As hateful as he found it to be, he could not deny or disbelieve the truth any longer. All his life he had rebelled against any power greater than he, refusing to bow his knee to a God who had the right to tell him what to do. Beelzebub was a god who could be appeased and manipulated, even tricked. A god like that could be figured out, and once understood, used.

But...Ahaziah suddenly wanted to scream. The awful realization shook his entire frame. *Beelzebub? He was nothing!* Only a cruel lie. In the deepest recesses of his soul, the sure knowledge settled that there was indeed a God in Israel, a God he had heard about and rejected. But even in the knowledge there was no turning, only a bitter hatred for the idol which had no life, and in the end had no power to help.

His lips drawn back in a vicious snarl, Ahaziah cursed bitterly his fate. And there on his royal bed, surrounded by the trappings of wealth and power, the rebellious King of Israel, according to the Word of God, died.

Jimmy Dollar, Evangelist

Brother Jimmy looked out the window of his personal jumbo jet, saw how close the wing tip was to the mountainside, and said a word Jesus wouldn't say. It took him a minute to remember he was supposed to be in the business of praying. The Tegucigalpa airport was surrounded by mountains, and landing a jumbo jet there was pretty hairy. It was necessary to go into what amounted to a dive as soon as clearing the mountain on approach, and to sort of slide right on down the side of that mountain, almost clipping the leaves on the trees growing on it. This dramatic approach was necessary in order to get wheels on the runway in time to stop the plane before reaching the end of the tarmac...beyond which waited a deep ravine...filled with rusting airplanes that didn't make it.

Brother Jimmy got down to business.

Getting down on his knees to pray was out of the question, so he compromised by cinching his seat belt so tight his legs lost their feeling, and gripping the arms of the seat with white knuckled fists and lifting his mellow voice to heaven. Others of his crew were also crying out to their maker to help them make it just one more time. There was a thump and the evangelist was thrown forward in his seat. They were crashing! Quickly, Brother Jimmy made the sign of the cross from his forehead to his heart. He wasn't Catholic, but he might as well cover all bases. Then he heard clapping, and looked up to realize that it wasn't a crash at all. The plane had landed, and the pilot was standing on the brakes to get the big jet stopped before that ravine welcomed them. The screeching of tires on the pavement could be clearly heard, and then the plane came to a shuddering halt. As it turned, Brother Jimmy could see the tail of some kind of aircraft sticking up out of the ravine, and he shuddered. He took a monogrammed silk handkerchief from the pocket of his monogrammed silk shirt and wiped the sweat from his forehead.

A miss is as good as a mile, he thought shakily. He unbuckled his seatbelt and tried to stomp some feeling back into his feet. He wondered if he should visit the bathroom in back just to make sure. You know how things show up on a white suit. But somebody else was already in there throwing up, so he decided he would just trust in the Lord and his spotless reputation.

As his plane taxied up to the gate, Brother Jimmy pulled a small mirror out of his bag and touched up his bleached white bouffant. He got it brushed back in place and sprayed it down with enough hairspray to set it hard as a cement block. Then he got out of his seat and took his white jacket out of the closet and shrugged into it. He tried to button it, but gave up when the button threatened to pop. Wouldn't do to put some TV reporter's eye out if that button decided to let go while he was being interviewed.

The press was waiting as the famous evangelist stepped into the open doorway of the plane and paused at the top of the steps to wave and give the cameras a shot of his good side. Descending the steps, he saw his second jumbo jet landing, the sudden billowing of black smoke as the pilot reversed engines and gave it all he had on the brakes. Brother Jimmy tensed a little as he waited for the plane to come to a halt. It held all the sound equipment, food supplies, cameras and other items necessary for a week's campaign in a foreign country. Brother Jimmy didn't like roughing it. His own personal chef was on that plane. His third jet, identical to the other two, painted white with a blue tail and white dove motif, had just started its suicidal dive down the side of the mountain. Jimmy Dollar Ministries was in four foot high teal colored letters on the sides. That plane held an entire mobile business office, with accountants, financial advisors, PR consultants and promotional experts, plus all the computers, desks, and communication devices needed to help them do their jobs. Brother Jimmy took his time coming down the steps, watching the last plane land. He couldn't relax until he saw the plane slow to a stop and turn into the off ramp. Mentally he calculated how much a new set of tires for three jumbo jets cost as he watched the cloud of black smoke rise in the humid air. Those tires had to be down to the rims after those stops.

He became aware of the stifling heat the minute he left the comfortable interior of the luxury jet. It rose off the tarmac to hit him like a fist. It came down like a weight from a pitiless brass sky. He was soaking wet by the time his white alligator shoes touched the blistering pavement. This was the downside to flying in your own personal plane, he realized. You don't get to pull up to the main terminal, where they send out one of those tubes to suck you right into an air-conditioned room. But then, the upside was, you got to make a dramatic appearance at the top of the stairs, just like the President on Air Force One.

He approached the crowd of reporters and waited until he was sure the cameras were on. Then he took off his Ralph Lauren shades and launched into his rehearsed speech. "People of Honduras," he began, "The Lord has sent us here to bring good news. He has shown me that he is going to prosper this country as never before." There was a smattering of applause from some citizens clustered around the fence separating them from the landing area, who heard his words over the loudspeakers attached to the microphones.

He lifted a diamond encrusted hand to wave appreciatively at the audience. "We will be in campaign for five nights in the beautiful soccer stadium your mayor has generously provided." If they only knew how much it cost us to rent that place they'd storm the mayor's office and string him up to the flagpole, he secretly thought.

He had been coached to say *futbol* stadium, but he just couldn't make the connection in his mind, and kept forgetting. *Football* was when the Dolphins and Cowboys butted heads, wearing helmets and enough gear to weigh a little guy down so he could hardly move. A bunch of skinny guys running their guts out continuously for hours around a green field, kicking at a little round ball - that didn't look so hard. *That* was soccer. Anyway, the translator they sent over with the news team cleaned it up for him, so no harm done.

"At the end of the week we will spend the weekend traveling around your lovely country, visiting in villages in some of the more unfortunate areas. Come to our meetings and I can promise you that your life will change. Remember, you can't reap a harvest until you plant a seed."

With that he waved again to the crowd and began to push his way toward the blessed air-conditioned terminal before the sweat started running over the tops of his shoes. To the members of the press, hanging on his every word with TV cameras whirring, he quoted some of his meaningless platitudes. Nobody could figure out what he meant, but it sounded good on the tube. People would watch and look at each other and say, "Oh, that is so deep."

It was deep all right. Only Brother Jimmy Dollar knew how deep. So deep that shovels should be handed out at his meetings. He knew something had gone out of him and he was just keeping up a show. Sometimes he felt cheap. But then he would look at his stretch limo, his drawers full of jewelry, his closet full of expensive clothes, and his five mansions scattered around the country, as well as the one in Cancun and the villa in France. Then he didn't feel so cheap. But there was something he used to have…it wasn't there anymore.

Inside the terminal he breathed deeply of the cool air and did a short interview, then the press was dismissed and he was ushered through customs to a waiting limousine. It wasn't a stretch like he was used to, but the A/C was blowing hard enough to almost knock a hair out of place, and cold enough to freeze the sweat on his face. With a wide grin, Brother Jimmy settled back and loosened his tie.

A little man in the front seat turned around and held out his hand. "Welcome to our country, Brother Jimmy," he said. "I am your cultural advisor and translator. My name is Alvarado Bustamente."

The evangelist leaned forward with some exertion and shook hands. "Glad to meet you, Al," he said expansively. He eyed the small, olive skinned man doubtfully. "I hope you can belt out a good translation of my sermons. I like to give it to 'em with all I got." Actually, he knew inside himself that his "sermons" had become nothing more than motivational speeches. Somewhere along the way he had lost the zeal that had made him an unusually effectual servant of the Lord. His fiery messages had touched thousands around the world via television. Now he was traveling the world putting the touch on people personally. When had he become no more than a carnival show?

As the conversation slowed, he reflected on his life. He had grown up poor on an Arkansas dirt farm, and hadn't owned a pair of new shoes until he started to school. He'd lived a simple life, content to live in a three-room sharecropper's shack and help his mother in the fields, earning enough to help feed his two little sisters, his mother and himself. He couldn't remember his father, who had died in a war somewhere. They had not had much, but they were relatively comfortable and happy in that little house. His mother had told them around the stove on winter nights about God, about Jesus and how he loved everybody so much that he died on a cross for the sins of the whole world. Her old family Bible was so worn that the pages would sometimes fall out as she read, but she made it come alive.

His bittersweet reminiscences vanished as the car pulled up to the Hotel Maya and a young attendant in a blazer hurried to open his door. His public face back in place, the smiling evangelist stepped out and started waving to the cluster of staff and management that had gathered to welcome him to their humble hotel. Some of them had no clue who the guy was, though his face was familiar around the world, wherever there was television. But he had rented the whole top floor of the hotel, so he must be somebody rich and famous. They had been trained to bow and scrape for *los ricos*.

The great man was ushered directly up to his suite of rooms, to leave the rest of his extensive entourage to spend the next hour getting registered and getting their room keys. He closed the door on the well-tipped staffer and went straight back to the shower. A complimentary silk robe was laid out for him on his queen size bed, along with a whole box of chocolates. Not bad for an ignorant Arkansas razorback, he thought, as he sank into the softest mattress he'd had in days, flicked on the television and drifted off to sleep to the drone of a Spanish speaking newscaster, who flashed a three second clip of the famous evangelist who had come to save the country.

Dreams came to Brother Jimmy in the night. They seemed real - so real he awoke and sat up in bed. The TV was showing endless scenes of *soccer* games. He turned it off and opened the chocolates. He knew it wasn't helping his waistline any, but it helped him think.

The dream had been a pretty accurate representation of his life at the time he had gotten saved. He was just out of school and working when he saw on TV where Billy Graham was coming to Little Rock. Coming from such humble roots, Jimmy had a fascination with famous people, and decided to go see Billy Graham at the stadium. At that crusade he had felt his heart strangely touched, as his mother used to say about the founder of Methodism, John Wesley. He had gone down to speak to a counselor that night, and made a truly genuine profession of faith. Sharing that newfound faith at work the next day, Jimmy spoke with such earnest conviction that three of his buddies came to the last meeting of the crusade and gave their hearts to Jesus also.

The dream had jumped to the years he had been a young preacher traveling from church to church, preaching the gospel and seeing new converts come to the Lord. He remembered the joy it gave him to see new souls born into God's kingdom, and how humble he felt to be the messenger chosen by God to tell them about the Savior.

But there came a time when he had risen to the heights of his ministry. The applause and adulation went to his head. A no-account country boy, receiving this much attention, as if he were really somebody special. And the way the money rolled in! Every evangelist had to raise his own support, not having a church to pay his salary, but he was raking in much more than a living wage. The money, too, began to go to his head. He convinced himself it was his due. He found scriptures to back up this idea that God wanted to bless him with riches, and he soon found himself preaching a message of prosperity, and only that message. It brought in money by the ton to convince honest hard-working Christians that God wanted to make them rich, if they would only plant seed in the ministry of Jimmy Dollar.

Suddenly the chocolates were leaving a bad taste in Brother Jimmy's mouth. Jimmy Dollar wasn't even his real name any more, he figured, than Binny Hinn was the name of Horace Dipstick, or whatever his real name was. He put the lid on the nearly empty box of chocolates, turned out the bedside light, and tried to sleep.

The next day Brother Jimmy Dollar brought the house down with his message of prosperity. Rich Hondurans hoping to get richer seeded the offering plates liberally, while many of the poor dropped in what few lempira they had saved to buy medicine and food for their families. The hopeless were drawn to the message of hope with a pitiful yearning for relief from abject poverty. The great man offered them hope. They planted all their seed in the great man's ministry, and the great man ate their seed.

For a week the roar of the crowd, the applause and adulation when Brother Jimmy would wave his hand and knock two rows of people flat on the floor drowned out the still small voice knocking on his conscience. Then, at the end of the week, Brother Jimmy visited the villages as he had promised.

The huge military helicopter descended with a roar and a cloud of dust into the clearing in front of the tin-roofed *tienda*, sending frightened children and adults running for cover in the little village of Chameleconcito. Residents watched fearfully from behind houses and trees as the giant beast settled and the rotor blades spun to a stop. They held their breath as a door in the side slid back. They expected to see a bunch of soldiers jump to the ground with weapons and blast everything to pieces. With surprise and curiosity they saw a large man in a tan safari shirt with pockets everywhere and khaki cargo pants start down a ramp that had been lowered. For the next hour the Honduran members of Brother Jimmy's evangelistic team went up and down from home to home trying to convince the folks that this was not a military operation, and the army was not going to blow them to smithereens the minute they showed themselves. Eventually a small group of brave souls began to ease into the clearing where the little church stood on the banks of the Rio Chamelecon.

The great evangelist had not come to preach the gospel. He had come for something the simple residents of Chameleconcito had never heard of. He had come for a photo op.

Brother Jimmy needed some photos of the poor and maimed, or something that would tug at the hearts of dumb but well-meaning supporters back home. He needed some video footage of himself holding a skinny baby with flies crawling over its eyeballs, or something just as shocking. He looked around at the people looking at him, many of them on their cell phones, calling friends to tell them to get over here and see if you can tell us what this is. He began to wonder if he was in the right place.

Then he saw what he needed, and it was coming toward him. A little old dried up man in a raggedy grey banana-stained shirt and tattered pants tucked into rubber boots hobbled over to him and shook his hand. The little man grinned, and when he opened his mouth, Brother Jimmy heard the cash register ring. He knew some rich dentists who would kick in a bundle when they saw pictures of him trying to help people like this old boy. Brother Jimmy put his arm around the bony shoulders of the old man and pulled him up close, putting on a sad, compassionate face as the video camera started to roll. He launched into his rehearsed speech about how the poor people of this humble little village had waited for centuries for proper medical and dental aid (and this old man looked like he might have been there at the beginning of the long wait), until the Jimmy Dollar team arrived with relief. Only it couldn't be done without the help of the faithful, like the loyal viewers who, for only a few hundred dollars, could…

Brother Jimmy at first tried to ignore the aggravating tugging on his jacket, but finally had to interrupt his spiel to see what it was the old man wanted. It might be something that would wring sympathy from some rich old grandma's heart. "Uh…what is it, Pop," he asked, and looked at Al the interpreter to translate, but the old man said, "I can spik Ingles, senor…I learn a few words while I am in jail, after they peek me up for try to enter the Unine Stase unlegal. It is why they send me to come tell you. Señor, I come to warn you of danger."

"Huh?" Brother Jimmy said stupidly. It was an unexpected statement that took a minute to penetrate his train of thought. "What do you mean…what danger?" He looked around at the peaceful scene and didn't see anything to worry about.

"It is the *ladrones*, señor…the ones from Guanacastales. They hear about the *rico* from the Unine Stase, and they come and steal you stuff."

Puzzled, the evangelist looked at his interpreter, then at some of the other Hondurans in his party. They all looked worried. They even looked scared. He looked around at the crowd of onlookers, and saw that they also looked scared. Most of them weren't even there anymore.

Now he was getting worried. He looked at his interpreter and said, "Would somebody please tell me what a 'ladrones' is? And what is a gwanna castle?"

172

Alvarado the interpreter was sweating. The pencil thin mustache on his upper lip trembled. His eyes were round and white. "These are very bad men he is talking about, Brother Jimmy. They came in and started blocking the road and robbing people on the way to the village of Guanacastales. They shoot people."

That last statement got through to the evangelist. "Okay," he said with sudden decision. "Photo op over. Everybody back to the chopper." He led the charge, walking as fast as he could up the rocky path toward the clearing. Cameraman, interpreter and all the rest behind him. Some of the villagers came along for the show. The old *campesino* hobbled along behind in their dust.

The pilot, who had stayed with the helicopter to guard it, was nowhere to be seen. The huge machine seemed to sit lower than before. Brother Jimmy stopped and stared. *The wheels were gone!*

Something was very wrong here. The short hairs on the back of his head broke free of the spray fix and stood up. The old man came limping up to them, breathing hard. Brother Jimmy was breathing hard himself, and it wasn't all because of the exertion. "What's going on here?" he asked the old man

The old man's dark, leathery face wrinkled in a grin and the words "dentist's nightmare" came unbidden to the evangelist's mind. "I don' know who get the wheels, hermano, but I see the policia go away with the long boat paddles on top." Brother Jimmy looked up and gasped. The rotor blades were gone! There went any hope of leaving this godforsaken place by air.

"Policia?" he said. "You mean the *cops* stole our rotor blades?"

"Si. They also take the radio, and the food, and one of the seats they put in the back of peekup truck. Look like you up the creek, Brother Jimmy." He shrugged and smiled at the cameraman bashfully. "A saying I pick up from the gringos in jail."

Brother Jimmy shook his head, trying to understand how this could have happened. He was just on a goodwill tour around the country, flown at government expense (after a hefty contribution to the president's reelection fund) in the giant helicopter. Now all the comforts, all the provisions and all safety measures were stripped away. Brother Jimmy suddenly felt very vulnerable. His fame didn't mean much at this point.

Everyone was milling around trying to figure out what to do when it was decided for them. A deafening shotgun blast roared from the edge of the trees and a heavy slug whanged off the side of the helicopter. *"Batita para que te quiero!"* the old man yelled (a saying that might be translated into English as "Come on, feet – do your stuff!"), and hotfooted it in the opposite direction from the shot. *"A la iglesia!"* somebody else yelled, and the whole group swept past Brother Jimmy, headed in the direction of the church. Suddenly he snapped out of it, realized he was standing in the open like Jungle Jim with a target on his back, and hot lead flying. He broke and ran after the others, indifferent to the damage done to his safari outfit when he snagged it diving over a fence.

The frightened group of visitors and locals huddled in the small church, wondering what to do. The mean guys were obviously not sure of themselves, or they would just come on in and kill everybody. "They must think we have military with us," the interpreter suggested. "The pilot was military."

Use of the word "was" sent a shudder through Brother Jimmy. He looked around. It seemed to him that the crowd in the little building had grown. Figures appeared in the doorway; a little old lady and a little girl came in. Then a man with a Bible in his hand came up on the porch. All of a sudden there was a full house, villagers taking seats and looking at Brother Jimmy expectantly. *Now* what was going on, he wondered. He looked at the interpreter, who shrugged. He looked at the old man, who grinned. Brother Jimmy wished he would stop doing that.

"Hermano," the old man said, "you are a preacher, no? The people hear there is a man of God at the church, and they come." He waved his hand at the people, silently watching Brother Jimmy. "They come to hear the Word of God."

"What about that gang of murderers outside?" Brother Jimmy asked. "Are these people nuts, thinking about a church service while guns are going off outside? We gotta think of something to do."

"Hermano," the old man said, "this is what the people do when there is trouble. They gather in the church to pray and to comfort themselves with the holy words of God." He took off his hat and lowered his head reverently. "It is all they have."

A light flashed on in the evangelist's mind. Something inside him came to a stop... and turned over. Then his heart thumped with life. "Well, why not?" he boomed. "Has anybody got a Bible in English?"

Reaching into his tattered and stained shirt, the old man pulled out a worn, taped together Bible. "King James Version," he said, handing it to Brother Jimmy.

This old man was full of surprises. Taking the Bible, the evangelist turned to John 3:16 and began at the most important truth he could think of at the moment. From there he moved on to the comforting words of the *Beatitudes*, his interpreter giving it all he had, and the people responding with enthusiastic amens. Into the night the service went. When Brother Jimmy's voice got weak, the praise team got up and beat out a rhythm on two turtle shells while another shook some maracas and the whole congregation sang.

Out in the darkness along the river bank, a gang of vicious killers listened and looked at each other in wonder. They lusted after the money they knew the gringo must carry on him. He was too fat and rich looking, and anyway, everybody knew all gringos were rich. But there were the shadowy figures of the guards around the little church to worry about. They might kill them all if they could see them clearly, but just as they were about to make up their minds to try it, more guards would appear. Big guys, too, and heavily armed.

One or two of the *ladrones* slipped away in the darkness, either from fear or from having their hearts touched by the spirit that seemed to emanate from the little church on the banks of the Chamelecon. As the night wore on, others tired of waiting and decided it was too risky. Those big mean looking guys surrounding the church would chop them to pieces before they got halfway to the door. Finally, they gave up in disgust and drifted away, disappointed.

As the sun rose over the muddy Chamelecon, the front door of the little church opened and the people began to emerge sleepily. Looking around, they found no danger, and slowly returned to their homes, laughing and talking about the wonderful message they had heard from the great evangelist. Someone had told them that he was famous in his country, and maybe in other countries too. After seeing how humble and sincere he was, and how powerful his message was, they could understand his fame. He was now famous in Chameleconcito, too.

Brother Jimmy walked out on the porch and stretched. His clothing was wrinkled, soiled and torn. His perfect hair was now ragged, plastered to his neck by sweat, but he was refreshed, ready for anything. If the thieves and murderers were out there, he would face them as best he could. God was in charge of him again, and he liked it.

Then someone told him the danger was over. The bad guys had for some reason left during the night. It was safe to travel the roads again, and someone had already called for vehicles to drive them out.

Brother Jimmy couldn't believe it. Five people had gotten saved during the night, and one lady had actually been visibly healed of arthritis. He had seen her hands straighten, and she had not been paid to do that.

He looked at the worn Bible he held in his hand. It had felt good to use it once more in the old way. What power it contained, and how that power seemed to flow into him again! He looked around for the old man, but didn't see him. No one could tell him where he had gone. Puzzled, he opened the cover to see if he could find a name. On the first page, there it was, right above a line put there for that purpose. There was only one word...

Gabrielle.

Mouth open, Brother Jimmy, the evangelist with a renewed heart, looked into the blue sky above the brown Rio Chamelecon, and hot tears stung his eyes.

The merciful God had guided his feet full circle.

He was back.

Stacked Deck

There I stood before Almighty God, not sure what to think. Was it a dream or was it real? I didn't remember dying.

The first rush of joy gave way to fear. Should I be there in his Holy Presence? In that brilliant light there was no place to hide the nakedness I felt keenly as my sins came to mind.

One after another I remembered them. Stealing penny candy in the first grade. Shoplifting as a teenager. Lying, so often and so easily. Letting others take the blame for things I did. Unforgiveness, anger, murderous thoughts that had once consumed me. Thoughts that I never felt were adulterous, but now could not deny. All the years of walking in the flesh, going my own proud way...ignoring the God who loved me.

What was the voice I heard accusing me, as I stood with lowered eyes? I knew I could not deny the charges, none of them. My accuser was right. All I could do was to agree with him, and confess.

"How do you plead?" asked the Judge.

With bowed head I answered: "Guilty."

Trembling, I waited with eyes closed for the verdict I deserved. I braced myself to hear the crash of the gavel. I wept for the evil of the days and the years I could never call back. But the Judge was in no hurry to pronounce my sentence.

"Is there counsel for the defense?" he asked.

My accuser objected loudly, which the Judge denied. I heard soft steps, like the scuff of sandals approaching the bench.

"Yes, Your Honor," a quiet voice said. "I am the counsel for the accused."

The accuser leapt out of his seat. "What evidence do you offer?" he screamed. "My evidence is irrefutable, proven without a doubt that the accused is guilty! He even confessed! The law in this case is clear. The penalty for this crime is death!"

At that point my eyes opened. I wanted to see the person who had stepped forward in my defense.

The appearance of the man was indescribable. I couldn't take my eyes off him. I couldn't tell you how tall he was, or the color of his hair. I only remember the air of confidence and peace about him, a quality that can only be described as… goodness. The eyes I do remember – so full of love.

"Yes, you're right, the law is clear," he said. "It is written that the wages of sin is death. This man is without excuse. He deserves to die."

"Then, what are you...?" the prosecution sputtered.

"But the penalty has been paid," my defender said. "The law has been satisfied." And he held out his hands, showing the marks.

"At age thirteen," he continued, "this one confessed and repented of his sins. He gave his life to me. I paid for his sins with the blood I shed on a cross. He is no longer guilty."

The prosecutor was an expert on the law. His devious mind searched feverishly for a loophole, and could find none. He could only stand frustrated and speechless. He jumped nervously as the gavel crashed down.

"Case dismissed!" announced the Judge.

My mouth was open in disbelief. The trial was over, and I was free! I looked at my Advocate. He was smiling at me. Then he turned toward the Judge, grinning broadly.

"Thanks, Dad," he said.

The Legend of Butch and LeeAnn

Take heed that ye despise not one of these little ones; for I say unto you, that in heaven their angels do always behold the face of my Father which is in heaven.

Matthew 18:10

We'll call her LeeAnn. She was born in East Tennessee into a church-going family. Beginning when she was three, she was sexually molested by every male member of her family - her grandfather, her brothers, brother-in-law and even her own father. Turning to her pastor for help, she was molested by him also. For all this she was twice sent away to girl's homes for incorrigibles. Her search for relief and some kind of happiness led her into a lifestyle of sex, drugs and alcohol. But deep in a secret place in her heart, she knew there was a God who could make her new. She made tentative steps toward him, but the testimony of worldly "Christians" held her back. Surrounded by the influences of the world, she was ready to give up hope. Suicide seemed to be her only way out. Then unforeseen circumstances brought her away from that environment and into a different sphere of influences.

It was as if an angel guided her steps...

Butch was not exceptionally tall for an angel, standing only nine feet eleven in his sock feet, but he made up for it in bulk. On assignments among mortals he didn't have to bend as low as other angels when going through doorways, but due to the width of his massive shoulders he invariably was forced to enter a room sideways.

Butch was among that select band of angels designated as guardians of children. At present he was on his way to the Throne Room to receive his latest assignment. The glittering pavement vibrated from the impact of Butch's hobnailed sandals as he double-timed it to meet his appointment. The last thing he wanted to do was to keep his Lord waiting.

He paused at the entrance of the Holy of Holies to check his appearance. He ran a thick, callused palm over the closely cropped stubble on his bullet shaped head and straightened his tunic. He pulled a wing around in front and tried to fluff the feathers into some semblance of order, arranging them so that some of the end feathers (the ones that he had accidentally clipped with his sword) would be covered. Wings were okay when you really needed them, but they sure got in the way in a knife fight.

When Butch was ready, the jeweled doors seemed to open of their own volition. He took a deep breath and stepped into the brightness.

The magnificent splendor of this room was always overpowering, even for an angel. Butch found himself wishing for a device invented by humans to protect their eyes from the sun, called Ray-Bans. He had worn them at times when he was on assignment in human form. He waited a moment for his eyes to adjust, then stepped toward the center of light and fell upon his face.

"O Father of Lights," he said, "I am reporting for my assignment. Your servant I am, as I am servant to the one to whom I am appointed."

The gentle answer came like a physical touch, softly strumming the angel's inner being. Butch's heart seemed to melt. He liked it here. He knew he was pretty rough-cut and homely, not at all like some of the astoundingly beautiful angels who served in other capacities. However, Butch wasn't at all bothered by that, figuring that God didn't need a glamour boy for the kind of work he usually handled. Sometimes it got pretty messy. Still, every time he was summoned to come into this place, Butch always got to feeling so good all over that he wanted to break out in songs of praise. But there were a bunch of other angels who hung around the throne all the time who already had that job.

"Come over here," the voice said. Butch jumped up and drew near the Source, so filled with love and so wrapped in pleasure that he was afraid he wouldn't pay attention to his instructions. He was glad he had been created able to look into the very face of the Almighty, something no mortal could do and live. As he waited for the Mighty One to command him, Butch felt no sense of urgency. He was in no hurry. He wouldn't mind standing right there in that spot forever, looking into that wondrous face and soaking up the endless waves of pure love that permeated the entire atmosphere. The face smiled, and Butch dropped to his knees, shot through and through with arrows of joy.

"I have a new assignment for you," the Lord said. "One that you will like, though there will be heartache enough."

With a brushing motion of his hand the Lord made as if it were a window in heaven, through which the angel could see a woman in a hospital on earth. She was on a delivery table, with doctors and nurses around. It was evident that she was getting ready at any moment to give birth. Butch smiled. He liked babies. He liked protecting them, and he was good at it.

"Judy is ready to have her baby," the Lord continued. "I want you to be there to make sure the delivery goes well. The enemy is down there walking to and fro. You will see to it that he does not devour this one."

God smiled again. "Her name is LeeAnn. Let her be as precious to you as she is to me. Remember to report back to me frequently." Then with an incline of his head, the eye of Majesty was directed toward the delivery room, and the Guardian Angel, having received his orders, streaked away with the speed of a light beam.

He arrived none too soon at the scene of delivery. At the very moment his feet touched the tile floor of the delivery room, he surprised a dark figure bent over the laboring mother, a misshapen figure that was not part of the medical team. A deep red, almost black, face looked up quickly as the air crackled with the angel's sudden appearance. Thick lips pulled back from broken yellow fangs in a feral snarl; the cloaked figure whirled to meet the interloper with a long, curved dagger in its hand. In that instant Butch knew that he faced a demon of death who had been interrupted just as he was locating the proper artery to cut, meaning to cause massive hemorrhaging that neither the mother nor the baby could survive.

Before the thought could even complete itself, Butch had instinctively drawn his sword and was closing with the enemy. Green eyes flashed with fear as the malevolent spirit slashed back and forth wildly with his wicked blade.

"You little puke!" Butch growled, circling cautiously just outside the demon's reach. "You picked the wrong kid to try to kill this time, buddy."

Whining with rage and fear, the slimy being cut the air with a powerful backhand swipe, leaving his right arm extended straight out from his body. With almost negligent ease Butch took full advantage of the opening and severed the arm at the shoulder with one clean sweep of his sword.

The noise of battle and the screams of the spirit being went unheard by the mortals in the room, but the tiny cries of the newborn were heard by all. The angel Butch, standing with one foot on the neck of his squirming enemy, in the act of pulling his blade out of the rib cage, heard the welcome sound of newly born life and grinned.

"Welcome to the world, kid," he said, wiping his blade on the huddled figure's cloak. "I'm here to take good care of you, and you're gonna be all right."

...

Time means nothing to an angel, as it means nothing to an eternal God, but on earth the years passed, and the little girl grew. Butch stayed pretty busy and he enjoyed his work. Many a malicious spirit felt the bite of his steel, and not a few unsavory humans found themselves in uncomfortable situations, not knowing how they got there. Because his Lord loved LeeAnn, Butch loved her too, and if it had been left up to him she never would have had even so much as a scraped knee or a childhood fever. He was zealous in the discharge of his responsibility – so zealous that many of the demons that normally preyed on weak and helpless children were beginning to steer clear of little LeeAnn. They had seen what happened to dozens of their foul brotherhood when they ventured within reach of the big angel's flashing sword.

Butch did his duty, but his first duty was to God. He reported to Him every day, receiving orders for each new situation. One thing that made Butch so good at his job, so dependable, was that he never acted on his own. He always did exactly what the Lord told him to do, no more, no less. Not that there weren't times when he wondered why he wasn't commanded to act, when it looked obvious to him that the child needed his help. It wasn't always the demons. There were times when he saw her falling and wanted to reach out and grab her before she hurt herself, but a quick glance heavenward failed to detect a signal to act. At such times he was forced to stand helplessly by and wince as the gravel, glass or some other dangerous object injured the baby (and later on, as she injured herself purposely). He often wondered why, but he never questioned the wisdom of God. He was content to just be a foot soldier and leave the planning to others. But it never got any easier to see the little girl get hurt.

One day, Butch followed the mother as she dropped the little girl off at her grandfather's house. The moment he entered the door, he felt the short hairs on the back of his neck bristle. He sensed the presence of demons. The air was thick with it. Immediately his hand dropped to the handle of his sword and he stepped to the little girl's side. But there were no malicious spirits near her. Puzzled, he looked around, alert for an ambush. His sword was half drawn, ready. But he saw nothing.

Then her grandfather came into the room, and suddenly every nerve in Butch tingled with eagerness for battle. Literally dozens of evil beings surrounded the older man, leaping on him, whispering in his ear, riding on his back, dragging at his feet. Butch shot a quick glance skyward, anticipating orders. He got a negative response. These demons were not attacking the little girl. They were all over the man, who was not Butch's responsibility. But then the angel looked into the old man's eyes and saw something that was so chilling, so alarming that he considered it an emergency. Faster than the speed of thought he was in the presence once more of his Commander-In-Chief.

Standing there in the full light of the Highest, Butch once again fought down the urge to just stand there forever and worship. He forced himself to remember the purpose of his hasty return to headquarters.

"Oh, Omniscient One," he said with bowed head, "you of course are already aware of the imminent danger to little LeeAnn, and have without doubt already decided what must be done to protect her. Let it not be an offense to your Holiness if I presume to anticipate...?"

Butch looked up inquiringly to see how his words were being received. Encouraged by the compassion he read in those gentlest of eyes, he plunged on.

"Of course, I just assumed that at the very least you want me to arrange things to get the child away from those lustful demons, but I thought I'd better make a quick check with you first. I mean, knowing how you feel about kids, and all, I almost went ahead and handled it myself, even though I've never done that on my own before." Butch gave an embarrassed little laugh. "I guess what I'm saying is that even though I knew you would approve of my doing something to protect the child, being as how a decision needs to be made pretty fast on this, I still felt that I'd better zip in real quick and find out which way you want me to go to spare the kid from this. After all, you might want me to, you know... the old man?" Butch said this as he laid one meaty hand on the hilt of his sword, while drawing the forefinger of the other hand across his throat.

Suddenly, as he looked into the eyes of God, Butch saw those eyes change focus and expression, looking past him at something beyond. Alarmed, Butch whirled to see, and his face went white.

"No!" he cried. "Oh, no – my Lord, you can't... you mustn't allow this to happen!" Butch dropped to his knees, imploring the Almighty to let him intervene.

But God's face was turned away from the carnal scene below. Tears streamed from eyes too pure to look upon sin. He spoke to Butch. "My faithful servant, because of your great love for the little child who is yours to protect, I will tell you this: I have chosen to give those whom I have created in my own image a free will. I will not force them to be either evil or good. How then would I ever know the wonderful gift of a freely returned love?

"I have entrusted the care and upbringing of this precious little one to her family. I have given them instructions on how to do it, but if they choose to disobey I cannot interfere. Not without taking away from them the choice and opportunity to have a true relationship with me."

Knowing when the demonically inspired act was finished, God turned his grieving face once more toward the confused little girl, who had gone back to playing children's games as if nothing had happened. Only now she had a new unseen friend clinging to her.

Heartsick and stunned, Butch turned to look also. He saw that one of the evil beings that swarmed around the old man had detached itself from him and attached itself to the little girl.

"That spirit of perversion will give the child much trouble in her life," said God, "and will make room for other evil spirits who will try to kill her. Your job," he pointed his finger at Butch, "is to preserve her life."

Butch felt helpless. "Is that all, Lord? Isn't there something else? Can't I just go and hack all those filthy creeps up with my sword, so she can be free?"

God shook his head. "Don't worry, Butch. You've always been obedient, not like those angels who once rebelled and were expelled from our presence. So, trust me on this. I have a plan. The little girl LeeAnn must go through a valley of trials because of the neglect and callousness of those mortals who were responsible for her. But I will be with her, and will bring her to an expected end. And you will be with her. After many days her path will cross that of some servants I am preparing to help her, and in the end she will be all right."

Reassured, but still heartbroken over what had just happened to the tender little one he was supposed to guard, Butch cleared his throat and mustered up his courage to ask for a little more clarification.

"Oh, my Lord," he said, "please forgive my questions, for no matter if I receive no answer from you I will still trust and obey. But... could I perhaps be permitted to know something more of your plan? If for nothing else, it would help me understand why I must keep my sword in its sheath instead of making mincemeat of all those filthy, slimy..." Butch caught himself losing it and shut his mouth in embarrassment. He bowed his head in defeat and let hot tears of frustration course down his cheeks.

A sound, as of a gentle breeze blowing in the trees, brought his head up. Again, he was looking, as it were, through a hazy window, and the winds of time were moving on earth.

"Behold," said God, "and understand."

Butch looked, and saw a man and a woman walking together on a country road. They laughed together. Then they argued violently. A strange couple, thought Butch, poorly fitted together. They went to church, and they went other places usually shunned by church people. Butch watched as a lifetime was compressed into moments, and children were born to the couple. They loved the children, and spent more time with them than usual, though Butch noticed several things they did that he thought he might have done differently. "But then," he sighed wistfully, "I'll never be a parent. So, what do I know?" As he watched, the children grew up and moved away, and the man and woman were left with empty arms. All their energy and attention had for years been focused on their children. Now they found themselves devoid of purpose and wondering about their future.

"They're looking for a mission," God explained. "See how they apply to first one and then another mission organization? They're seeking my will for their lives."

"But, Lord... what's that got to do with little LeeAnn?"

"All right – I'm going to do something I don't ordinarily do. I'm going to let you see a little of what the future holds for your little one." God waved his hand, and Butch saw LeeAnn literally immersed in every form of perversion and rebellion, sinking deeper and deeper until finally she came to the point where she could no longer bear the pain of her self-destructive lifestyle. Something in her heart cried out to be rescued.

"In the end she will not be saved by the sword," God explained. "These, as imperfect as they may be, are the instruments I will use in steering LeeAnn toward the abundant life I meant for her to have."

"What?" Butch blurted it out before he realized how it sounded. "Them?" He pointed at the man and woman, now older and alone, sitting on a porch reading. The woman was sipping on a 20-ounce Diet Coke and the man was scratching under his arm and eating a bowl of homemade ice cream, while occasionally looking up to watch a humming bird buzz around.

Butch scratched the stubble on his head. He looked doubtful. "Well... the woman there – maybe she has some possibilities. I can tell she's way too smart and beautiful for him though. Why, look at him – sitting there mindlessly shoveling that whole gallon of ice cream into his dumb face. What a slob!"

Butch warmed to his subject. "The guy doesn't look like he has over two brain cells to rub together. I bet if his brains were dynamite he wouldn't have enough to blow the hat off his head. Check out that vacant look in his eyes." Butch shook his head dubiously. "I don't know, Lord. This dude..."

He became aware that God was patiently drumming his fingers on the arm of his throne chair. He had an indulgent, if slightly bored, look on his face.

"Are you through?" God asked. Butch fell silent. He ducked his red face and dug a toe at a golden tile on the floor.

"You're right about the woman," God said. "She is too good for the poor 'slob' as you call him. But she has been through a furnace of affliction and persecution from other Christians, and all this without losing her trust in me. As a matter of fact, her faith has only grown stronger, as has her wisdom in dealing with matters of the heart and emotions. Her compassion knows no bounds, but she will not compromise with sin. She can help LeeAnn as no other to discern the difference between right and wrong."

"So," Butch cut in hopefully, "the dumb looking dude there – he really doesn't enter the picture? He's just so much excess baggage maybe...?"

"Not at all." God smiled at Butch's picturesque way of expressing his thoughts. "This fellow may not look like much to you – and I'll grant you he isn't exactly a spiritual giant – but he has one all-important quality that is just the thing LeeAnn has missed, and needs."

Butch raised his eyebrows inquiringly. This had better be good. He trusted God, but he was beginning to wonder if the Lord wasn't letting his kindness and mercy overrule his better judgment here.

"What is that quality, O Lord and King?"

God placed his hand over his breast. "He has a huge hole right here," he said. Butch looked puzzled. The guy had lung cancer, or a heart bypass or something? Maybe some kind of a hernia? Couldn't be much of a hole, or else all that ice cream the guy was packing in would leak out.

"The hole I'm talking about," God said, knowing Butch's thoughts, "is the vast emptiness he feels now that his children are gone. He has no focus in life since there are no longer any little ones in his care.

"And that alone," God explained, "is the one quality he needs to serve my purpose. This is going to be the easiest job he ever had."

God chuckled at the simplicity of his plan. "LeeAnn, you see, never experienced the safe, pure, sacrificial love of a father. She was abused all her life by most of her family members, including her father. The way I have ordained the family, it is the father I have charged with demonstrating my love to the others. LeeAnn will never be able to make progress toward loving me until she has been shown my love through a flesh and blood father."

"You mean to tell me," Butch stuttered, "this lazy..."

"I'm not nominating him because he's industrious," God interrupted, "but because he is ready, willing and able to be a channel for my love to LeeAnn."

Butch mulled it over. "Yeah – I guess if you can see that in him I'll have to go along with it. I knew all along you would know better than me. I guess after I got a look at the jer... uh, the guy you're puttin'all your hopes in, I just needed a little reassurance. Thanks." He grinned and rubbed his chin. "The beautiful thing for this lucky bozo," he said, "is that in order for him to do exactly what you want him to do, all he's got to do is just – exactly nothing."

"Now you've got it," God said. "All he's got to do is let my love flow through him to this little girl, whom he will come to think of as his little girl. And in the end, she will have the relationship with me that I always intended she should have."

Contented and satisfied at last, Butch the guardian angel flew back to renew his vigil at LeeAnn's side. Countless times his heart was broken, and countless times, but for the warning look he saw as he beheld the face of God, he would have drawn his sword to put a swift end to the degradation of LeeAnn. But in the passage of time two paths were slowly merging, until a day came when east met west.

And they were there under the benevolent eye of God, the wounded and disillusioned young woman full of yearning, and the older woman with the wisdom to repair broken hearts.

And an older man, with nothing but a father's aching, empty arms.

The Qualifying of Zeno Sodd

His hangover could only be described in nuclear terms. Splitting the atom was nothing compared to the pain that was splitting Zeno Sodd's skull. The corporate business meeting had turned into an all-night party, which he had finally left at around three A.M. He staggered down the hallway to his room, heart pounding, out of breath. After three tries he eventually got the key card to work, and entered his room just as it began to spin. He missed the bed on his first try, and floundered around on the floor for a minute, before hoisting himself up with the help of a hotel chair. Steadying himself, he aimed a finger at the bed with one eye squinted, and lurched forward again, this time landing safely, face down on the cool softness of the mattress.

But sleep didn't come immediately. The amino acids from the garlic cheese hors d'oeuvres he had ingested at the party, combined with the free-flowing champagne he had guzzled, were setting off ten-megaton explosions in his head with every heartbeat. He fumbled for a bottle of antacid on the lamp table and got the lid off, dumping three or four tablets into his mouth and chewing them up. He also swallowed a couple of Tylenol and lay back, waiting for the blessing of sleep to claim him. After a while he finally drifted off, and in his sleep he dreamed. And his dreams were bad.

Zeno dreamed he died.

At first Zeno didn't know what to think. He opened his eyes and sat up, confused. Everything seemed the same, but somehow strange. Everything was too quiet. He looked at the clock on the bedside table. It had stopped at four o'clock sharp. He got up, went to the window and swept the heavy curtain back. It was daylight, but all he could see was a bright mist, like a fog outside. He looked around his darkened room. Everything seemed slightly blurred, like the fog had penetrated here, too. He shook his head to clear it, not liking the thought that was creeping in. Was he...dead?

"Well, hey," Zeno said out loud, slowly accepting that it might be the case. "It's not like I expected to live forever." Always philosophical, he shrugged his shoulders and told himself that he had no complaints coming. "I've lived good, and had a few laughs here and there," he murmured, and mentally listed his accomplishments and qualities. I gave my share to charity, he mused, and I treated folks right when they deserved it. I worked hard, climbed the ladder and made a success in business. Maybe I stepped on a few hands on the way up, but hey – that's business. So, all in all, I guess I haven't done too bad. Nobody can say ol' Zeno hasn't earned his reward.

He took another look around, sucked in a deep breath and realized the hangover was gone. Maybe there was something to what the preachers always said about the afterlife. He felt himself, pinching his fleshy jowls, patting his expansive belly. "All there, and sound," he said wonderingly. He felt fine. But it was just too quiet.

Okay. If I really have bought the farm - and it appears that I have - there are things I have to do. Zeno was proud of his organized mind, and set to work packing his suitcase for the trip to heaven. He wanted to be squared away when the angel came. The bag was a Gucci design, with expensive leather and gold hardware. Zeno packed it with all the things he figured he would need where he was going, closed and locked it, and picked up the phone.

"Hello, is this the front desk?" he inquired cheerfully when a female voice answered his call. "Look – I don't know a good way to say this, so I'll just go ahead and give you the news...this is Zeno Sodd, in room 13, and I just died. I was wondering if you have a special elevator, you know...going up?" In his altered reality, it made perfect sense to believe that a fine hotel would have such a luxury service for their preferred customers. He congratulated himself for thinking of it.

"What's that...? No, this is not a joke! I told you, I'm Zeno Sodd. You should know I'm a regular here. I spend a lot of money with you people. On the level now," he said, curbing his indignation, "I really have kicked off, right here in my room with no warning. Looks like the Pearly Gates for me. So, if it isn't too much trouble, would you mind sending down the special elevator? I know you must have one, you know, the one that goes to that big penthouse in the sky?" Zeno liked his new way of thinking.

"Certainly, sir," the desk clerk said, only a hint of amusement in her voice. "That will be the central elevator in the hallway, the one marked "Express." Be sure you don't get on the one to the right or to the left. Only the central one will take you where you want to go."

Zeno thanked her and hung up the phone. "Chee," he said under his breath, "they oughtta train these clerks better than that."

He grabbed his suitcase and lost no time vacating the room where he had breathed his last. He hastened down the hall whistling cheerily. His gait could be described as a confident strut. Zeno didn't anticipate any trouble with the transition. Matter of fact, he was looking forward to the mansion he had heard about, and spending all his time on the golf course, without all the stress he got from abrasive colleagues every day. He stopped at the elevators and read the sign over the central one. "Express," he chortled. "You the man!" And he punched the button.

He tapped his foot while he watched the floor numbers light up over the elevator in descending order. The bell dinged, and the gleaming elevator doors slid ponderously open.

And Zeno Sodd very nearly jumped completely out of his skin! He recoiled at the gory sight that assaulted his eyes on the interior of that central elevator. From floor to ceiling, blood was splashed everywhere. It was smeared on the walls, and puddled on the floor. Crimson streaks spattered the ceiling. The shock was tremendous. Zeno felt his knees giving way, and grabbed hold of the wall to steady himself. What hellish evil had happened here? A serial killer, or a mob hit? A scene from a movie about a chainsaw massacre flashed through his mind.

Zeno's traumatized brain was trying to get a message down to his trembling legs to run, when an object inside the blood-drenched elevator caught his attention. It was a red-stained post, or something, leaning against the back wall of the elevator. It had a crossbar at the top, and there was a scrap of paper attached to it. There was writing on the paper, too small to read without getting closer. Zeno was terrified, but he felt compelled to at least take a look. Perhaps it was a clue to what this horrible scene meant.

He swallowed nervously and, with care not to touch anything, he leaned in to see if he could read the note. "I am the way, the truth, and the life," it said. "No man cometh unto the Father but by me."

That was all.

Zeno passed a trembling hand over his perspiring face. He wasn't sure what the note meant, but he knew his nerves were shot. He began backing away, stepping carefully backward, away from the bloody elevator, until his shoulder blades touched the opposite wall. "H-holy begonias!" he croaked. "One thing's for certain...ol' Zeno's not about to set foot on that elevator! There's gotta be another way!" Briefly, he considered the other two cars, but by this time he was thoroughly spooked about elevators. Desperately, he threw quick glances up and down the hallway.

"There!" He spotted a sign over a door labeled "Stairs." Quickly, he snatched up his bag and charged down the hallway. Gingerly, he eased the door open and peeped in. A sense of relief washed over him when he saw there was nothing on the other side of the door but a flight of stairs. He leaped up the stairs, taking them two at a time. "Now this is better," he muttered, confident in the strength of his rather stout legs. This way he could be sure to get where he was going. "Legs were made before elevators anyway," he quoted. No telling what would have happened to him if he had gotten on that elevator. He shuddered at the thought, and shifted his bag to the other hand as he settled down for the long climb.

Zeno's Reception

In the process of time, Zeno surmounted the last flight of steps and staggered out a door into a world of surpassing beauty, alive with streams of brilliant and colorful light. Momentarily out of breath from the long climb, Zeno sat down on something soft and fluffy to recover his wind and scope out the scene. He looked around in open-mouthed amazement. This was like nothing he'd ever seen, or imagined. The lights and the colors were indescribable. His heart leaped when his eyes came

203

to rest on a looming, bejeweled wall, stretching into infinity both ways, and right in front of him a huge gate, the only opening. The gate was of solid pearl! Rising above the gate Zeno could see the tops of gleaming buildings, made of something that appeared like gold…a glittering city of light!

"Far out!" Zeno cried, and leaped up with eager anticipation. He made it to the gate in a stumbling run, impatient to be inside. Disappointed when the gate didn't open of its own accord to admit him, he beat on it with his fist. "Hey, open up in there!" he ordered in his most authoritative Dale Carnegie voice.

He waited while nothing happened. He banged and yelled again, but with less bluster this time. Again, there was only silence. This wasn't helping Zeno's self-confidence any. It couldn't be possible that nobody was home. He raised his fist to knock again, but hesitated while the moment lengthened, and the silence thickened. It was so quiet Zeno could hear the thumping of his heart. A slow trickle of sweat started down the side of his face, sliding down his neck to be absorbed by his shirt collar. He loosened his tie and took a couple of deep breaths. Something just wasn't right. He felt his flesh beginning to crawl.

"MAY I HELP YOU, SIR?"

The deep voice boomed from directly behind Zeno, and it turned him inside out. He performed a heroic flat-footed leap, did a one-eighty in midair, and landed crouched in what he probably thought was a karate fighting stance, on trembling legs spread so wide he was almost sitting. Head tucked down into his shoulders until his ears touched his collar, he held his clawed hands up in front of his face, ready to meet the threat. The word that exploded involuntarily from Zeno's mouth was not quite in harmony with his present surroundings. His bulging eyes darted back and forth like a startled deer in the headlights.

He sustained somewhat of a shock at the sight of a tall bearded man in flowing white robes, who stood regarding Zeno with gentle eyes. Zeno was certain the man had not been standing in that spot only a second ago.

"W-where did you come from?" Zeno croaked. His Adam's apple bobbed up and down as he labored to swallow. "W-who are you, anyway?"

"Sir;" the man said solemnly, spreading his hands in an expressive gesture, "I am popularly known as Saint Peter, but that's not the important thing. The question is – who are you?"

"Wha... who am I?" Zeno's jaw dropped. Unbelievable. Things weren't going at all as well as he expected here. He'd always thought that they had their stuff together at this end. Files of information and records on every single human on earth. Wasn't there supposed to be some kind of book? Surely somebody up here had gotten an email or at least a sticky note that Mr. Zeno Sodd, important executive in a major corporation, was on his way up.

"You see, sir," the man explained, "This is not the kind of place where it is necessary for one to walk up and beat on the gate for admittance. One can enter freely here through a door that is always open when certain qualifications are met. I'm afraid that the credentials you would need..."

"Aw, is that all?" Zeno laughed nervously, his worried expression giving way to a relieved grin. "Man, if you wanted credentials why didn't you just say so right up front?" Quickly, he bent to undo the tie on his Hefty Bag. Strange...he could have sworn he'd started out with all his stuff in some kind of suitcase... Oh, well. Zeno rummaged around in the depths of the bag. "Okay, let's see here," he mumbled to himself, digging through the clutter. "Credentials, credent...ah, here it is!" He straightened up brandishing a nine-by-twelve gold leaf picture frame, with an official looking diploma behind the glass. He held up the frame for St. Peter to see, and tapped the glass with a manicured fingernail. "See the name of the school on this diploma? I was a Rhodes Scholar, man! Graduated with honors." He didn't see any reason to mention how much he had paid a guy to take the tests for him. "Got one of these from Yale, too."

Warming to his favorite subject (himself), Zeno dipped again into the bag. He came out with a checkbook, and flipped it open for the gatekeeper to inspect. He looked both ways and leaned in to speak in low, confidential tones. "Not many people know this," he said, almost in a whisper, "but I've got a Swiss bank account!" He grinned smugly, waiting for the guy's eyes to widen when he saw the amount of his balance.

But the man paid no attention to the amount, nor to the checkbook for that matter. He waved it out of his face. "Sir, these things are not..."

"Wait! Just wait a minute!" Zeno held up a hand and jostled things around in his bag. He saw that this guy was going to be a tough sell, but he had trained all his life to overcome the resistance of a reluctant customer. He had no doubt that he could wear the man down before he was through showing him his stuff and delivering his song and dance. He was good at this.

"Just hear me out, is all I ask," Zeno said, reaching down inside the bag again. Why in blazes was everything in a Hefty Bag? He came out with a thick portfolio full of papers. "I know you guys gotta have certain standards up here. I understand that, and today I will settle your mind on that score, and convince you that I meet all those standards. I have spent a lifetime accumulating knowledge and possessions and honors." Giving St. Peter no time to respond, he opened the folder and took out a photo. "You want recommendations, I got recommendations. I've got a whole folder full of them. Letters and awards from big shots all over the world. Heads of state, even. Look, see this photo? See who I'm standing beside, shaking hands? That's the President! He signed that for me personally. How about that, huh? And here's one from…well, hey, just take your pick…"

Zeno's rapid-fire chatter tapered off as it dawned on him that the man wasn't listening. He had his arms crossed and his eyes were rolled upward as if he had heard all this before. Zeno felt another little check in his confidence. What was it going to take to impress this guy, anyway?

He decided he was going to have to hit him with his big guns. He didn't like to do this with just everybody. Secret things didn't stay secret long if you began to noise them around to every Tom, Dick, and Harry. But, duh…if you couldn't share a secret with Saint Peter, who could you trust? Again, he looked around to make sure no one was listening before turning back the lapel of his jacket. "Look, friend, I didn't expect to have to go into things that are best kept secret, but now that I think about it, you probably have one of these, too." He pushed the lapel out, so St. Peter could clearly see the little gold pin he wore.

"I'm a Mason, buddy," he stated with pride. "That oughtta stand for something." Then he leaned close and whispered the grand omnific secret word in St. Peter's ear.

"Well, now," Zeno said pompously, "I think we're through here." The gatekeeper had no choice but to honor that ancient and universally revered word, and admit him into the celestial lodge. With an air of dismissal, he picked up his bag and started to shoulder past the man.

The hand that restrained him was neither forceful nor threatening, but at that light touch upon his arm, Zeno's legs lost their strength and refused to function. He blinked uncomprehendingly. Nothing of what was happening to him fit with anything he had ever learned through his experience in dealing with people and getting things done. He felt a sudden embarrassing urge to cry.

"Fella, listen…" he pleaded, "This is insane! What more proof do you need before you realize that I'm an all right guy who has earned the right to go through that gate you say is always open to anyone who has the proper qualifications?" Zeno's eyes narrowed suspiciously as he stared hard at St. Peter.

"You know, I'm beginning to wonder a little about you, mister." He put his hands on his hips, like a schoolmaster preparing to reprimand an unruly student. "Is this your regular job? Why, in the movie I saw about heaven – with Jimmy Stewart or somebody – the guy they had watching the gate wasn't quite as picky as you are about who got in. I thought you loved everybody up here."

St. Peter released a patient sigh. "Yes, sir, we do love everybody up here." His face was sad. "Inside those walls there is nothing but love. That's why nothing of sin can enter in. It would corrupt everything here like it did on earth. Since there is only one remedy for sin, the qualification for entry that I was referring to has to do with our spiritual condition..."

Zeno suddenly smacked his forehead with the palm of his hand, startling St. Peter. "Why, what's the matter with me?" he blurted. "Of course! I should have known you guys up here would be mostly interested in religious stuff! Laughing nervously, he shook his head at his own density. "I must be losin' it," he said, "but wait just a minute." He held up a finger and bent to his Hefty Bag once more. Underneath everything else he closed his hand around a little suede jewelry box. You had to get up early in the morning to get ahead of old Zeno.

He opened the box and held it close for St. Peter to peer inside. "There's twenty-five perfect attendance pins, one for every year I never missed a Sunday at Church and Sunday School. Even when we went to the lake on weekends, I always had the wife or one of the kids read a piece out of the Sunday school quarterly, so naturally I counted that on my attendance record." He produced a folder full of documents. "Here, you can check out my W-2 forms and see how much I shelled out to the church." He riffled through some more papers for anything that might help. "Let's see...baptismal certificate, deacon ordination...oh, here – here's my church letter, saying I'm a member in good standing, and all that." Somewhat smugly, Zeno jabbed a finger at the letterhead. "I know you're familiar with the name of this church. Biggest in town, services on TV every Sunday, nationwide. Note the denomination." He gave St. Peter a knowing wink. "We both know this is the only denomination that's going to make it, so I'm not worried about that." He took out a handkerchief and wiped sweat off his face, then continued rummaging in the bag until he got to the very bottom. "I even got a Bible in here someplace – ah...here it is!" He held up a worn, plastic covered Bible and waved it in the air. "My dear old mother gave me this, God rest her soul. I had it shrink-wrapped to protect it."

Proudly, Zeno arranged all these trophies in a semi-circle around his feet and stood back with a triumphant smile. He crossed his arms over his chest. "Well, whaddaya say to that? Think that'll about do it, chum?" St. Peter wagged his head patiently. "Sir," he said, "I think we can clear up the misunderstanding more quickly if we just get straight to the heart of the problem. Let me see your feet?"

Zeno just stared at him for a moment. "Huh? You want to see my feet? What do my feet have to do with anything?" His face was a study of puzzlement as St. Peter stepped over and lifted one of his feet, inspecting the sole of his shoe. With tightened lips, he put that foot down and lifted the other foot while Zeno steadied himself with a hand on his shoulder. He put the foot down and dusted off his hands, a grim look on his face. Gentle sorrow was in his eyes as he shook his head.

"What? What was that all about?" Zeno demanded. "What did you look at my feet for? What did you see?"

"Many things. Worldly things. Tar, dirt, bubble gum. Other...stuff. You really should watch what you're stepping in, you know. But I saw no blood."

"BLOOD?" Zeno squawked. Visions of the gory elevator flashed across his mind. He shuddered involuntarily. He couldn't stand the sight of blood. This was unreal. Why was this happening to him? If this guy knew what a weak stomach he had, he wouldn't be talking about blood! "Why should I have blood on my shoes? Yuck! That's disgusting!"

"I'm sorry, Mr. Sodd," said the saint. "It's not my rule, but His. If it were just me, I might be impressed enough by your obvious attainments to go ahead and admit you. But, when you think about it, His way is really better. This way, everybody has an equal chance to make it, not just those like you, with money, education, political pull, and strong legs like yours." His mouth relaxed into what might be taken as a smile. "Of course, they might find riding in that central elevator slightly offensive to their sensibilities."

St. Peter's tone changed perceptibly. "You know, it cost Him dearly to provide that elevator for you." In the gatekeeper's

211

eyes there was a flicker of painful memory, personal and haunting. "It may not look so pretty, but neither is sin. Sin is a very disgusting stink in the nostrils of God. The ultimate result of sin is death. Of one thing you may be certain, Mr. Sodd…the blood you saw in that elevator is the only sinless blood that ever was shed. It was willingly shed to pay for your sin." He pointed his finger in Zeno' face. "That precious blood, which you so haughtily disdained, is the only thing that will pay your way through those gates!"

Zeno wilted under the stern impact of those words. But the man wasn't finished. "You detoured around the only provision there is for entering in here. You had contempt for it. You thought you could do it better your way, and climbed the stairs under your own power. Yet now that you are here, before the very gates of heaven, you see that you have no power of yourself to open them. Go ahead and try, if you wish." He stepped aside and gestured for Zeno to approach the gates.

Zeno found he could not take a single step in that direction. His feet would not obey the command of his brain to move. In that moment, his pride, his pompous ego nosedived. It felt like there was a chunk of lead in his stomach. He felt sick.

"Your achievements, your awards, all the symbols of earthly glory are commendable – on earth. You have earned the respect of man for the work it took to accumulate these awards. But good works, even works we do for God and man, will not earn admittance through those gates. So, you see, since you rejected the only method by which you can enter here, the baubles you have brought here believing they would buy your admittance, are nothing but...a bag of garbage."

Those words, though spoken gently and in a spirit of love, cut Zeno to his soul. But they rang true. He was shriveling visibly, the weight of guilt bowing his shoulders. He opened his mouth, but had no words. The gatekeeper spoke instead.

"How do you think it makes Him feel, Mr. Sodd? For you to reject his provision for your redemption, sent to you at so great a cost. He didn't pour out his life's blood just for the fun of it." The gatekeeper struggled for a moment trying to think of a way to explain further, in a language Zeno would understand. It was an enormous thing, but so simple. He decided that Zeno had by his own admission been regular at church, so he should have had plenty of opportunity to hear the simple gospel. Perhaps he would be circumventing the will of God by trying to explain further to a man who had already died.

"No, Mr. Sodd, I'm afraid I have explicit instructions to admit through these gates only those who have His blood on their feet. And you can only get that blood on your feet if you go by the way of the cross. You didn't choose to go that way, believing your way was better. There's nothing more that can be done for you. I have no choice but to bid you good day."

With that, St. Peter sadly turned and silently disappeared into the mists.

Zeno was devastated. This could not be. All he had worked for, all he had become – wasted! Why had not someone told him about these things? Or...had he perhaps...not listened?

Blindly, he stumbled back to the elevators, uncertain what else to do. He pressed the button with a shaking finger and stood waiting numbly. His mind was blank, unable to function, to think, to plan.

He was in a daze when he boarded, and the elevator started down. He was dimly aware of another person in the elevator with him, operating the buttons. It wasn't until he heard a hollow chuckle that Zeno was brought out of his fog and looked up. The first thing he noticed was that the button marked "Basement" was the only one lit up. Then he noticed the guy was looking at him out of red-rimmed eyes, flashing a wicked grin. Zeno did a double-take when he saw what the man was wearing. Weird getup, Zeno thought. Must be going to a costume party. Now who would he be impersonating, in a pair of red long johns and carrying that dangerous looking pitchfork? In that outfit, he looks just like pictures I've seen of the old ...!

At that moment, Zeno woke up.

"Aaaagghhh!" He was screaming as he fought his way out of the dream. "He's got me! He's got me!" he shrieked mindlessly, flailing his arms wildly, throwing covers everywhere. "Help me, somebody, help me!"

He sat bolt upright in bed as full awareness came flooding back into his mind. He was in his hotel room. He had had a nightmare. It had been a shockingly real dream. The smell of brimstone was still in his nostrils. His body was clammy with cold sweat and he had the shakes. But he was alive, thank God!

Thank God?

Suddenly, Zeno knew the meaning of his dream! Many, many souls had died without a prayer, but Zeno knew he had been given a second chance. And this time he was going to take it!

He flung off the covers, jumped out of bed and dressed quickly. Excitement flowed through his veins like electricity as he took long strides down the hall. His color had always been blue, but that had changed now. His new favorite color was crimson. Zeno Sodd was on his way to make his reservation for that central elevator, the one that was decorated in a beautiful bright red!

The King Who Became A Carpenter

In Heaven the King of Kings stepped out of the impossible light of the throne room, where he had been in earnest conference with his Father. Making his way through the gleaming outer courts, he took note of the gathered multitudes of resplendent and adoring Cherubim and Seraphim, who shouted and sang his praises as they bowed and fell back to clear a lane for His Majesty to pass before them. Exiting into a shimmering street of pure molten gold, he was met by an even more deafening acclaim from the throngs of angelic beings who immediately clove to his side, each treading on the others as they jostled for position. Those in back stood on tiptoe, craning their necks to get a glimpse of the face they lived to look upon. And, one by one, each of these towering, powerful warrior beings, clamoring for all the world like little children begging for treats, was rewarded in turn by full eye contact with his Commander-

In-Chief. The incredible communication of all-satisfying love and approval was mutual.

Abruptly, the King slackened his brisk pace and paused before a portal at once real, yet mystical, through which objects and movement could be seen but dimly, vaguely obscured as though veiled in mist. Turning, the Most High gathered his royal robes around him and beckoned for silence. In his hand he held a gilt-edged scroll.

"My beloved," the words rolled out into the sudden hush. "In my hand I hold a commission. I must leave you now for a time..."

The ensuing roar of shocked disapproval was so loud and so long that the King finally had to raise both hands high and signal once more for silence.

"I have a commission," he continued when the cries of denial had subsided. "In the Councils of Heaven, it was decided before time began that, as the Earth groaned and travailed in sin, one must be sent from these realms of glory to redeem mankind."

The waiting legions held their breath as the King lifted his eyes and let his gaze slowly move from splendor to splendor. There was nothing in sight that was not composed of precious gems, gold, silver, pearl, and a brilliant shimmering light bathing all with radiance. As far as the eye could see the atmosphere was charged with excitement and activity. In the distance, trumpets and other musical instruments sounded. Choirs spontaneously burst into angelic songs of praise. It was as if all the heavenly host found it impossible to keep silent when the King walked abroad. And near at hand the legions of warrior beings, terrible of aspect and armed for battle, fell on their knees in worship as their Sovereign assigned certain duties to the archangels Gabriel and Michael, and to others of the angelic hosts, who immediately departed on their missions. Then, with a word of farewell, the Majesty on High turned and disappeared through the portal.

All heaven fell silent in awe of the Plan that was manifesting itself on Earth. And in the stillness, they heard faintly, as if from a great distance, the cry of a newborn baby.

The fullness of time had come.

...

In the close confines of the stable, the warm air was thick with the earthly smells of animals and dusty straw mixed with manure, as well as the unwashed bodies of shepherds who had crowded in to see. The young mother, a humble peasant girl, cradled the babe in her arms and gazed lovingly into his face. She held her thoughts in her heart. Her husband stood by, thinking his own thoughts, pondering the astounding facts that had been revealed to him about this child. What must it have been like where he came from, the husband mused, shaking his head in wonder. His finite mind, he was sure, would never be able to fathom it. He looked down at his rough-palmed, scarred carpenter's hands and felt the enormity of the task he had been entrusted with – raising, training, and providing a home on Earth for the Son of God!

The years were swift, the life was hard. The child grew in favor with God and man, and became a man himself, with the rough, calloused hands of a carpenter. He labored and was tired. He ate his bread in the sweat of his brow like any man, and slept the sleep of exhaustion at night. That he was exceptional, all were aware, but he was accorded no special privileges. Like everyone else he was expected to fulfill his obligations as a son and as a worker, as a useful member of society.

Then, for three brilliant years he received the acclaim of men. He was hailed briefly as a king, but even that failed as the persecution began. Hardly a follower was present at the end, when a cruel wooden cross was thrust up against a muddy sky, and the Son of God, who had left behind the unimaginable splendors of heaven to become the Son of Man, now became the Savior of all mankind.

The King who became a carpenter did it all for me, and for you. In heaven he was worshipped and adored day and night. He gave that up to come down in the dirt with us. He ate our humble bread with us, he slept on the ground beside us. He suffered and bled and died, and he didn't have to do it. But, by what he did, and how he did it, he proved that he is a God at hand, and not a God far off. He identified with us, and is able to understand what we go through. He spoke our language and got his message across.

And we, as we go out into the world to spread the Gospel, who do we think we are to complain that there is no air conditioning in the villages, or that the food is not what we're used to, or that we have to sleep on a dirt floor? Are we better than the Lord who called us to go where the people are? If the God of Heaven and Earth could humble himself to become one of us, then surely we can stretch our comfort zones and adjust ourselves to other cultures enough to effectively communicate the Good News to those who are waiting to hear it.

In learning to be cross-cultural missionaries, we can find no better example to follow than Jesus, the King who left his Kingdom to become a carpenter. Jesus Christ - the King who walks and works beside us – the great cross-cultural missionary of the ages.

<u>DRIVEL (100% PURE)</u>

Cop Fun

Sterns and Watson relaxed in the front seat of their black and white police cruiser, which was parked in front of a Dixie Cream doughnut shop. On the seat between them was a box of fresh-out-of-the-oven mixed doughnuts with the lid up. Orson Sterns, white male, 25 years old with a receding hairline, was behind the wheel, due to his lack of seniority. His partner, Beulah Watson, slumped comfortably against the passenger side door with her arm out the window, enjoying the late spring air. Watson was 30, black, and married with two kids. She was about the same height (five-seven) as Sterns, but weighed considerably less. With a paper napkin she dabbed at a smudge of white cream filling on her chin and took a sip of coffee from a Styrofoam cup. The night was young, but she was already bored. The doughnut run might turn out to be the high point of their shift.

Sterns licked his fingers and brushed at some white powder on the front of his black, well-stuffed duty shirt. He turned and rummaged in the box, carefully nudging a couple of chocolate-covered doughnuts aside. He knew those were Watson's favorites, and he only ate those when he wanted to irritate her.

"Any more of them blueberry-filled ones?" Sterns mumbled, still chewing the remains of the first. He found what he wanted, sighed contentedly, and sank his capped teeth into the delicious sugar-coated muck. He finished the doughnut in three bites, licked the purple goo off his fingers, and washed it all down with the steaming coffee. He was reaching for his third sugar hit when his partner tapped him on the arm.

"Hey, Orson, check out the redneck," she chuckled, inclining her head toward the skating rink adjacent to the doughnut shop.

Sterns lips tightened involuntarily at her use of his first name. He preferred to be called "O.J." (J for Jewel), or simply, "Sterns". What kind of image did a name like "Orson Jewell" give a tough, savvy cop?

He looked in the direction Watson indicated. There was no mistaking the guy she was referring to. A hulking shapeless mass of hair and tobacco stained denim leaned against a 50s vintage rusted out Chevy pickup with a cracked windshield and tobacco-streaked, dented sides. In his best police academy style, Sterns began trying to classify the dude. The subject, that is.

Dang! Why couldn't he remember the proper terms? A cop who put "dude" on a report would be laughed out of the station.

The subject was about six feet tall – hard to be sure, the way his body was slumped over the tailgate of the truck. Anywhere from 25 to 40 years old, white, probably – the built-up dirt and grease on him made it hard to peg his race. Definitely male, with a beard like that. Shaggy black hair bushed out around the edges of a greasy camouflage hunting cap. There had been an apparent attempt to shave one side of the fat jowls, but the job hadn't been completed, giving a lop-sided look to the face. Dull, lifeless eyes and a pendulous lower lip drooling tobacco juice down the front of his filthy bib overalls strongly suggested a family tree with few, if any, branches. About two inches of hairy ankle showed between the ragged ends of his pants legs and the tops of his brogans.

"Okay – I give up," Sterns said. "Vegetable, animal, or mineral?" They both chuckled.

"Yeah," Watson quipped, "I don't know whether we should call in rabies control or the city garbage collection service." They cackled at that. Maybe the doughnuts would score second on the fun meter after all. They both reached for another doughnut and settled back to enjoy themselves.

The doors of the skating rink were suddenly flung open to disgorge a noisy, colorful crowd of teenagers, many with rollerblades and skates flung across their shoulders by the laces. The rube came to life as two blondes came his way, pony tails bobbing. They were walking fast, in animated conversation.

Bubba Sneed was caught by surprise at first, and slow to react. He withdrew a forefinger from his right nostril and wiped its high yield product on the front of his overalls. He lurched to his feet and lifted his cap as the two females passed him. The movement caught their attention. They ceased talking and just stared at him as they walked by. Bubba tried throwing them a grin. His mama always said his grin was a sight to see.

The girls flinched in unison and looked at one another. Their pace quickened. They got in their car and sped away before Bubba got a chance to speak to them.

He shrugged, swiped a mop of matted hair out of his face, and resettled the cap on his head. Shifting his chew into the other cheek, he spat over into the littered bed of his pickup. Them girls was too talky anyway. He'd try a different approach on the next one.

A tall brunette in pink leotards and black shorts came out alone, fumbling in her purse for her keys. Bubba hitched up his overalls and stepped boldly in front of her. "Hey, purty thang! Do yew lak babies?" he said.

Astonished, the girl froze. She stared nervously at the hulking figure blocking her path, as if she didn't understand what he had said. Or what he was, for that matter.

Bubba waited, grinning hopefully. At least the gal hadn't lit a shuck like the other two. Must be she liked him. He wiped tobacco juice off his mouth with the back of his hand and shifted his feet. The girl must have misinterpreted his move. Instead of car keys, her hand came out of her purse clutching a can of pepper spray. She let Bubba have a liberal shot of it right in the eyes. He jerked back, surprised. He pawed at his eyes and sniffed his fingers. Then he licked them.

"Hey, 'at ain't bad," he said, blinking rapidly. "I rekin yew must be Metsikan. I lak Metsikan salsa, an' I lak Metsikan gals..."

She wasn't interested. Carefully, the girl inched around Bubba, keeping him at arm's length. She looked at her can of pepper spray in disgust, and tossed it over her shoulder. Then she beat a path to her car and was gone.

Sterns and Watson watched all this from their squad car, uncertain as to what, if anything, they should do. It wasn't often they found this much entertainment on their beat. It seemed a shame to break it up. They were already so interested in the little comedy unfolding before them that the doughnuts had been forgotten.

"Whattaya think, Sterns," Watson said, chuckling. "Do you think the guy's dangerous?"

"I don't know," Sterns laughed. "Let me call the zoo. Maybe if I can describe it, they can tell me what it is, and if they've had one escape. Then maybe we'll know if it's dangerous."

Watson cracked up. "Yeah, or maybe we oughtta get the curator of the anthropological museum down here to take a look. What we got here could just turn out to be the Missing Link. Hey, Sterns, we could be famous."

They were on a roll. They watched with anticipation as a group of about twenty youth gave the hayseed a wide berth, keeping a distance of at least thirty feet between themselves and the unsavory looking character. The crowd split in the middle, flowing in a wide circle around Bubba. No one came close enough to speak, or to catch anything.

"Whoa! Lookit that!" Sterns remarked with a snigger. "The hillbilly musta cut some serious cheese to fan the crowd out that far!" They both collapsed in helpless laughter. Watson gave Sterns a reproachful slap on the shoulder, wiping tears from her eyes.

When she had recovered her breath enough to talk, Watson straightened up and said, "Okay, maybe we should remember that we're cops, and go on over and at least check the hair factory out."

They got out of their car and walked across the parking lot. They did their best to straighten their faces and look serious as they approached the skaggy looking hick, who had let down the tailgate of his pickup and was sitting on it scratching in his beard.

"Good evening, sir," Watson said in her best cop-eez. "How are you tonight? Everything okay here?"

Bubba looked up. "Uh, yess'm," he said, snatching off his cap. "I figger I'm goan do real good tonight."

"Oh?"

"Huh?"

"Well...explain that. What do you mean when you say you goan do real good tonight?"

Out of the corner of her eye Watson could see Sterns's belly begin to jiggle. She gave him an unseen kick on the ankle.

"Hey," Bubba said, looking from one to the other, "y'all po-lices don't think I'm doin' sump'n wrong, do you?"

Well, I might find a point or two to criticize about your technique, Sterns thought to himself.

"Uh, that depends," Watson said. "Suppose you go ahead and tell us what you got going out here on this parking lot tonight."

"Jus' doin' what my mama tol' me."

While Watson engaged the subject in conversation, Sterns quietly checked the interior of the pickup for evidence of weapons or drugs. He didn't see anything but empty Red Man pouches and crumpled McDonalds containers. There were plenty of scattered fries and bits of uneaten cheeseburgers, but nothing that looked illegal. Disgusting maybe, but, unfortunately, that wasn't against the law.

Sterns shined his maglight over in the back of the truck. Piled in amidst the other clutter were some old car batteries. Now those might could be used to construct some kind of bomb. Suddenly Sterns was all business. With all the emphasis on terrorism these days, you couldn't be too cautious.

Keeping a hand close to his holstered service revolver, Sterns said, "Sir, would you step away from the vehicle, please, and show us some I.D?"

"Huh?" Bubba's finger paused on its third trip to his nose since the officers had confronted him.

"I said, do you have any I.D?"

Bubba looked puzzled. " 'Bout whut?" he said.

Sterns and Watson looked at each other. "Do you have a driver's license?' Watson asked.

"Oh, sure." Bubba reached in the pocket on the front of his bib overalls and brought out a laminated card that looked like it had rusted. He handed it to Sterns, who held it gingerly between thumb and forefinger and rubbed at the brown tobacco smear with his thumb. A likeness appeared which could have been no other than the individual they were interviewing. Sterns made note of the information on the license and said, "Okay, Bubba..." (that was actually the name on the card) "Maybe you better go ahead and explain what you're doing out here tonight. The people coming out of the skating rink seem to be doing their best to avoid you for some reason."

Watson thought she could tell Sterns the reason for that, as she moved to a more upwind position.

"Well," Bubba said, "my mama been thinkin' she ain't goan live forever. She taken a notion I needed me a wife to take care of me after she gone. I's just out here lookin' for me somebody to marry up with."

Watson loved romance. "Having any luck?" she asked.

Bubba checked the nose again, in case he hadn't mined it thoroughly enough.

"Had me a coupla bites," he said. One little gal I ast to marry me said, 'In your dreams, sleazewad.' I ain't sure what that meant, but I think she was innerested."

"Wow." Watson pulled out a tissue, wiped her eyes, blew her nose.

"Yeah," Bubba said. "Ain't love beautiful?"

Sterns was beginning to get nauseous. "I heard you ask one of those girls if she liked babies," he said. "What was that all about?"

"Oh, I gotta make sure the gal I marry don't want no babies." Bubba shrugged. "Don't know why exactly. Sump'n my granny used to say, I guess."

"What was that?"

"Whut wuz whut?"

"What was it your granny used to say?"

"Oh, that. Well, my granny used to say to my mama, 'If that boy ever gits married, you better pray he don't never have no kids'."

Watson was thoughtful. "Excuse us for a minute, will you, Bubba?" she said. Taking Sterns by the elbow she drew him aside.

"I don't know about you, partner," Watson said, "but it doesn't look to me like we have anything to be concerned about here. Ole Bubba here is obviously running on a low-watt bulb. If he's a threat to anybody it's the City Beautiful Commission. Maybe we should make some more rounds, then cruise by here in a half hour or so just to see how our boy makes out."

"My sentiments exactly," Sterns agreed. We haul this guy in just to get him off the streets we'd never hear the last of it. Ol' Bubba may belong in a dumpster, but not in jail."

Watson wrinkled her nose. "Besides," she said, "I don't want him changing the ambience of our squad car. I'd never be able to touch another doughnut."

They turned back to Bubba, who was stuffing another wad of Red Man into his whiskered cheek. "Hey, Bubba," Stern's said. "We're tired of messin' with ya, so we're outta here. Good luck to ya, man. Oh…One other thing…"

"Yeah? Whut's that?"

"If you find a girl tonight who wants to marry you, let me know, will you?"

"Uh – sure. Why."

"Oh, I just wanna prove something to my partner here. She doesn't believe in miracles."

Bad Bob

Bad Bob swaggered through the batwing doors and the room got suddenly quiet. Every eye turned toward the six-foot-four, 280 pounds of hair, muscle and dirt known all over the west for his violent temper and his speed with a gun. Nervously, every eye watched Bad Bob shove his way through to the bar, where he stomped a muddy boot on the rail. "Whiskey!" he ordered.

The bartender, a scary looking individual in his own right, hesitated, trembling. He knew he was out of the good stuff, the expensive liquor he kept under the bar for his special customers. Did he dare offer Bad Bob anything less than the best?

What the heck, he decided. A guy that mean has probably drunk every kind of poison. He'd never know the difference. The bartender set a bottle of the regular stump water on the counter – then went white when he saw the look in Bad Bob's eye.

"Okay, I – I'll just run out and buy a good bottle," he stammered hastily. "It won't take a minute!"

Bad Bob shot him.

Nobody in the saloon moved a muscle. Bad Bob walked over to a table where some miners were playing poker. "What're you guys drinking?" he growled. He snatched a shot glass from a grizzled miner's hand and tossed the drink off in one gulp.

"Gahh!" he roared, flinging the glass across the room, where it ricocheted off the powdered brow of a saloon floozie.

Bad Bob spat and wiped a dirty sleeve across his mouth. "You boys oughtta know better than to drink mule sweat like that!" he snarled, and shot all five of the poker players.

The dancehall floozie marched up to Bad Bob, rubbing her forehead. She was mad. "Hey, buster," she fumed, "what do you mean, throwing things around like that? Don't you know you might put somebody's eye out?"

Bad Bob shot her.

He looked around. Nobody was left in the saloon except some cowboys who had been sitting at a table talking to the floozie. One of the cowboys looked mean. He shoved his chair back and got up, a dark look on his weathered face. He squared off at Bad Bob, flexing his fingers over a low-slung holstered pistol. He was a shaggy haired man in wooly chaps, his square chin covered in blue stubble. Without further warning, he went for his gun. Bad Bob shot his bullet in mid-air.

The cowboy stared, dumbfounded. While his slow-moving brain was struggling to process the amazing fact of two bullets meeting in the air, another bullet from Bad Bob's gun arrived along the same path as the first, and got stuck in the cowboy's gizzard.

While the cowboy lay croaking, one of his friends lurched to his feet from behind the table. "Yew dirty no good horn-swogglin' dog breath load of sheep dipped skunk guts! Thet was my buddy you shot. Draw!"

Bad Bob shot the cowboy's leg off. The cowboy hopped away on one leg, still cussing. He apologized to his other friends at the table as he left. "I gotta go git me a band-aid or sump'n' fer this here stump, boys," he said. "Then I got me a little practicin' to do!"

By this time Bad Bob was beginning to feel slightly irritated, so he just went ahead and shot everybody else in the room. What the heck. If he was going to have to drink slop he'd just as soon drink alone.

The bat-wing doors creaked, and Bad Bob whirled, six-shooter cocked.

Through the door stepped a gangly youth, wearing thick glasses, a ragged yellow shirt and baggy checkered pants held up by a pair of red suspenders. Worn out shoes two sizes larger than his feet flopped clumsily across the floor. Bad Bob shot him.

That is, Bad Bob shot at him.

It happened that just as Bad Bob's finger tightened on the trigger, the too-large shoes shifted, causing the hick to stumble slightly. The bullet whipped by his head with millimeters to spare.

Bad Bob was appalled. Since he was ten years old and killed all his politically correct family, along with their livestock and pets, he had never missed a shot. He took steadier aim and drilled the kid again.

Only the kid had bent to tie his shoelace, and the bullet only snipped the clasp off the back of his suspenders.

But there was nothing slow about Bad Bob's reflexes. Even as the bullet was leaving the barrel of the gun, he realized he had fired where the kid's belly button had been a split second before, and immediately he thumbed the hammer again, this time aiming a little lower.

As the hammer fell something spanged against the gun barrel. The punk's suspenders had snapped loose and shot over his head like a giant rubber band, hitting the gun with just enough force to deflect Bad Bob's aim a couple of inches. The slug missed the kid's heart as he stood up. It whipped between his side and left arm, continued on through the thin wall of the saloon, and killed a Dominecker hen out in the street.

Bad Bob ground his teeth, snarling profanity. "You ignorant hayseed!" he screamed. "Don't you know I'm Bad Bob? Why are you still standing there after I've shot you three times?"

The skinny kid clutched at his pants to keep them from falling around his ankles. His face had gone white. The thick glasses slid down his nose. He pushed them back in place with a trembling finger.

"Uh...I guess I'm too scared to run," he said. His voice trembled. "You're really Bad Bob?" he asked.

"Yes, you freaky broomstick!" yelled Bad Bob. Frantically he cocked his revolver again. "Now get ready to meet all the rednecks in hillbilly heaven, you...!"

Flame spurted from the barrel of Bad Bob's gun. Only now he was getting rattled, and his timing was really off. The kid had let go of his trousers with the intention of shaking the notorious gunman's hand, and his trousers had fallen around his feet. At the exact moment the gun went off the hayseed was in the act of bending to pull his pants up. The bullet passed over his body so close it snipped the button off the trap door of his red long johns.

Seeing he had somehow, incredibly, missed again, Bad Bob went berserk. He began madly fanning his six-shooter, which probably had no more than fifteen or twenty shots left in it. When the cloud of blue smoke lifted, the dumb kid was standing there unharmed, holding his pants up with both hands. Bad Bob whimpered with frustration. Why couldn't he shoot this kid? He looked at his gun hand. It was shaking badly. He had been shooting with his right-hand gun, which was empty now, so with a strangled cry Bad Bob went for his left hand gun. He was desperate to shoot this kid, or he would never be able to hold up his head again.

The twerp, as it happened, had grown up idolizing Bad Bob. "Gee, Mr. Bad," he said, "you're my hero. I've always wanted to meet you and shake your hand!"

Bad Bob's finger was taking up slack on the trigger. The need was intense in him to shoot this stack of bones. His nerves screamed for the kill.

The kid's clumsy right hand reached out to shake at that precise moment and, as luck would have it, he bumped Bad Bob's gun hand, turning his left wrist inward just as the gun went off.

"Dang!" Bad Bob groaned through gritted teeth, looking down at the bloody front of his shirt. "This is really bad," he mumbled, "Right through the old bread basket." He dropped his gun, staggered across the floor and slumped over the bar, breathing heavily. "Hey, kid," he whispered hoarsely to the dumbstruck youngster, "come closer. I wanna tell you something."

The kid leaned over to hear Bad Bob's last words. Bad Bob grabbed him by his scrawny neck and slammed his fist right in the string bean kid's long nose. The kid staggered backwards across the room and crashed into a table, knocking it into kindling.

Bad Bob managed a weak smile as he slid limply to the floor. "Now I can die happy," he wheezed. "I finally hit the hillbilly."

Poke Chop and Mean Mickey

Something was wrong at school. Poke Chop could sense it the minute he walked into his classroom. Everything was too quiet.

Everyone looked at him as he squeezed through the door and dropped his book bag next to the specially made, extra-large, reinforced bench and table he used as a desk. The bag didn't make a thud when it hit the floor, the way it should have had it contained books. Poke Chop never put books in his book bag. It was filled with food.

Puzzled, he looked around at all the moon faces staring at him. He wiped his face to see if he might have egg on his chin. Up at the front of the room, Miz Norkelfitz slouched at her desk calmly shuffling papers in preparation for the start of the school day. Nothing seemed out of place until he noticed several of the kids nervously shifting their gaze over to one side of the room.

He craned his neck to see what they were looking at. Then he did a double take.

Over on the other side of the room sat a new kid...only Poke Chop wasn't sure it was a kid. It looked more like a throwback to the Stone Age. The...*thing* was almost as big as Poke Chop, and his bullet head was shaggy with stiff dishwater colored hair that looked like something somebody pulled out of a mattress. His face looked like it had been rescued from a washing machine after the agitator had done a little work on it. He had a square chin and little beady eyes under bushy eyebrows. His stub of a nose looked like it had been pushed to one side to make room for something that never arrived. And – Poke Chop stared - was that a blue shadow of beard on the kid's chin. Whoa! This kid must be the record breaker for years in the third grade. Poke Chop himself was working on his third year under Miz Norkelfitz (they called her Snorkel for short), and she had told him he was definitely going to graduate up to the fourth grade this year. She was tired of him sneaking her lunch out of her desk drawer every day and eating it.

The new kid looked pretty rough in every line. He was built like a barrel with legs, and his arms were long and muscular, with tattoos. He wore an armless tee shirt with "Eat More Wimps" printed on the front. He had on a pair of cargo shorts that came to below his knees. His legs were short and knotty. His tennis shoes looked too big for his legs.

Poke Chop took all this in with mild interest, then his eyes moved back up to the guy's face. Poke Chop stopped scratching his armpit for a second. The throwback was looking straight at him!

The kid had a wicked grin on his face, showing crooked snags of teeth. He was methodically smacking one ham-sized fist into his other palm.

Poke Chop mulled it over and shrugged. New kid in school. So what. It wasn't something Poke Chop could eat, so he quickly lost interest and pulled his health studies book out of his desk, turning to a dog-eared page that had pictures of nutritious food. He was daydreaming about food when Miz Snorkel rapped him on the head with her ruler.

"Poke Chop, what's the matter with you, boy?" she asked. "I done axed three times for everybody to turn in they homework for last night. Where yours at? And don't tell me yo' dog done ate it!" she said, wagging her ruler like a finger in his face.

Poke Chop ducked his head, embarrassed. "No'm," he said, so quietly she had to strain to hear him. "My dog ain't ate my homework. I...I done ate it myself."

Miz Snorkel just stared at the boy while the whole class laughed. "You done *what?*" she said in unbelief. "I know you ain't...ar-unt telling me you went and ate yo' homework, boy! What in the world make you do a thing like that?"

"Well," Poke Chop squirmed in his chair, "I didn't want to go in the kitchen and open the frig, because the door squeaks

241

and I might wake up Mama. So I rummaged around in my book bag and found my homework all folded and…"

"And what?"

"Well, in the dark it just looked so much like a samwich…"

The class was in an uproar by this time, and as the laughing died down he heard someone say, "What a dork." He looked around for the source of the comment and saw the new kid looking at him again with a sneer.

Poke Chop felt a tap on his shoulder and turned around. PeeWee Smith leaned up from the seat behind him and whispered, "Better watch out, Poke…Mean Mickey says he's gonna get you at gym time."

So that was his name. Mean Mickey. Had a ring to it. He wondered if Mean was his first name, or Mickey.

At gym time all the girls were at one end of the gymnasium kicking a soccer ball around, and all the boys were playing basketball. All except Poke Chop, who had taken an earlier opportunity to filch another kid's lunch out of his desk, and was sitting on the bottom bench of the bleachers munching away when Mean Mickey walked up to him and squared off, hands on his hips.

"Hey, Fatso, he said, "whatcha doin' settin' there shining the bleachers instead of playing ball with the rest of us? You think you too good?"

"Oh, hi, Mean," Poke Chop said around a mouthful of ham and cheese. He wiped mayonnaise off his right hand and extended it in a friendly gesture. "We ain't met yet, but somebody tole me your name. My name ain't really Fatso. It's Poke Chop. You can call me Poke if you want to, like everybody else."

Mean Mickey slapped the hand away and snarled, "You makin' fun of me, boy? Why, for two cents I'd yank you off that bench and render you into a bucket of lard."

Poke Chop reached into his watch pocket and pitched Mean Mickey two pennies. Now truly enraged, the new kid reached and grabbed Poke Chop by the bib of his overalls and gave a mighty jerk, the muscles in his biceps making the hula girl tattoos dance. His intention was to sling this fat grease ball across the floor so hard and fast he'd be like a bowling ball when he hit the group of boys, knocking them down like tenpins, showing them who's boss. A sudden pain shot through both shoulders.

Mean Mickey looked up from the floor to discover that the bowling ball was still sitting there on the bench, calmly licking mayonnaise from his fingers. When Poke Chop grinned his eyes almost disappeared in his face. "You lookin' kinda funny, layin' there with yo' arms all twisted out like shoelaces or sump'n."

Mean Mickey was furious. He started to get up and felt the pain in his shoulders again. His arms wouldn't work. He discovered with a shock that he had dislocated both shoulders. He felt like a grasshopper pinned to a scientist's display board.

But with a name like Mean Mickey to live up to, he wasn't going to let a little thing like two dislocated shoulders and a sea of pain slow him down. Rolling back to thrust his short legs as high as he could get them, he suddenly kicked down in an S curve, snapping his back off the floor and landing on his feet. Grinning like he really enjoyed having two arms hanging useless like limp spaghetti, Mean Mickey walked over to the bleachers, got his right arm jammed down in between the seats and twisted his body suddenly. Poke Chop heard a loud pop, and Mean Mickey raised that arm and flexed it. He turned and repeated the process with the other arm. Sweat beaded his face but he was still grinning. He popped a fist into the opposite palm and said, "Okay, fat boy...now that I got my flippers working again, let's you and me dance."

Poke Chop blushed. "Gee, I dunno...ain't it supposed to be boys dancing with girls? Boys ain't supposed to dance with boys." He got off the bench and stood there wiping his hands on his bib overalls. "Say, Mean," he said, "you got anything left over from lunch? I'm gettin' kinda hungry."

Mickey couldn't take it any longer. He knew how to handle anger; he knew how to handle fear. Those were his stock in trade. But indifference he couldn't handle. The other kids were watching now, all in a circle, staring. He had to make his mark on this mountain of fat or he would lose his standing as top dog in the schoolyard. He might even lose his bullying

244

license. Taking a look around at the expectant faces, he spat on his right fist and picked a spot right in the middle of Poke Chop's expansive belly. Then he swung. It was the mother of all breadbasket punches. He gave it all he had, driving his fist like a pile driver into Poke Chop's belly.

His arm sank in to the elbow, but Poke Chop didn't fall. He looked puzzled. "Hey, man, whatcha tryin' to do?" Reaching down into the top pocket of the bib of his overalls, he came out with a handful of Oreos. "Man, you almost crumbled my dessert."

Mean Mickey was frustrated. For once he wasn't creating the fear and terror he always liked to see in his victims. He did some rapid recalculations. He wasn't getting anywhere trying to intimidate the fat boy. He'd swung with all the power in him and his punch hadn't phased the guy. If you can't beat 'em, join 'em, his daddy always said.

Suddenly Mean Mickey laughed loudly, and the crowd of goggle eyed boys jumped collectively. He slapped Poke Chop on the shoulder and said, "Hey, man, I was just joking, heh, heh. Just wanted to see what you had in you." To himself he thought, and what you had in you must be an entire supermarket.

"Hey, Poke," Mean Mickey said, steering his new buddy toward the door, "let's you and me go get some chow, whaddaya say? I got a whole locker full of groceries I made these other wimps pay me with, just for the privilege of staying alive for one more day at school."

Poke Chop grinned and licked his lips. As the two walked off together, arm in arm, Mean Mickey was heard to say, "Man, you and me can run this place...if you don't eat it down to the foundations first. We gonna be good buddies. Hey, did you know my great-grandaddy was Bad Bob? Ever hear of him?"

Ol' Shep

Old Shep awoke, sat up on his favorite sleeping rug and yawned widely. He shook himself all over and indulged in a long, satisfying morning scratch behind the ear. Then he trotted over to the door wanting to go outside. His size had not been considered when the pet exit had been installed, but he was able to squeeze through without too much difficulty.

Outside on the lawn, Shep urgently sought out his favorite bush and hiked his leg on it. That bit of business disposed of, he scratched dirt and grass over the spot and trotted off in search of adventure.

For breakfast Shep turned over a neighbor's garbage can and ate the remains of a child's takeout Happy Meal. Then he resumed his daily route, circling through the backyards of the residential section, where something interesting almost always turned up. He drooled with anticipation.

A high board fence barred his way. This presented no problem for Shep. Gathering himself, he leapt the fence with ease. A fluffy overweight cat sunning itself on a back deck came awake, bounded straight up in the air and came down facing in the opposite direction, squalling loudly, sprinting for the nearest tree. Shep was right on the cat's tail, deliriously happy. He kept the terrified animal treed until a beefy looking woman in a pink housecoat and curlers in her hair stepped out the back door and hit him behind the ear with a thrown shoe.

Yelping with pain, Shep fled, ducking under a broken board into another yard. Missing no opportunity to investigate a new arena, he sniffed out a pile of garbage bags left on some steps. He chewed holes in all the bags, sorting carefully through the litter until he was certain there was no food to be had. Disgusted, he finally wandered off in search of more lucrative sport.

After covering the back yards in the residential district, Shep trotted toward the business section of town. As he passed a bank, he felt a sudden call of nature, and left a sizeable deposit on the sidewalk in front. A cursing rent-a-cop chased him away.

It was time for a mid-day nap. Shep cruised around until he found what he was looking for. A utility crew was working amidst a circle of orange cones. He crawled under their truck and fell instantly asleep in the cool shade, knowing instinctively that the truck would not be moving until five o'clock.

Shep dreamed he was chasing a rabbit. His body twitched. He uttered little growls in his sleep. Before long, the weird sounds emanating from underneath their truck attracted the attention of the utility crew. One of them crawled out of the little canvas sun shelter they had been resting in and came over to investigate. "Hey, fellers," he called, "c'mere!"

The others put down their coffee and donuts and ambled over to have a look. They bent down and peered under the truck. Every time Shep twitched or let out a yip they punched each other and laughed.

Suddenly Shep snapped awake. He sat up too quickly and bumped his head on the truck's muffler, which set the men into a fit of uncontrollable laughter. Some internal clock had triggered an urgency in Shep. He was supposed to be somewhere, and at a certain time. His daily life was ruled by routine. Once a week, as regular as clockwork, there was one place he always visited. If he didn't hurry he was going to be late!

Scrambling out from under the truck, Shep raced down the street. Frightened pedestrians jumped out of his way. Heedlessly, he cut across traffic, almost causing a pileup. His tongue was lolling, dripping saliva by the time he arrived at a conservative one-story brick and glass office building near the medical center. He loped up the steps, triggering a sensor as he approached the entrance. Automatic glass doors slid open and Shep went inside. A lot of people were seated in plastic chairs in some kind of waiting area. They stared at Shep. Paying them no mind, he trotted around the reception desk and went down the hall to the right. He seemed to know exactly where he was going. He passed two doors and stopped at the third. It was closed. Shep scratched on the door and whined.

A man with a goatee wearing a white coat and thick glasses opened the door. He looked down at Shep and smiled. "Well, here we are," he said, "Right on time, as usual. Come on in." He held the door wide as Shep entered with a happy, drooling smile. Going straight to a leather covered couch, Shep jumped up onto the plush cushions, turned around three times, and finally settled into a comfortable ball.

The man opened a drawer of his desk and took some things out. Then he walked over and took a seat in a wingback chair next to the couch. He crossed his legs and laid a yellow legal pad on his knee. Thoughtfully, he tapped a pencil on his teeth. "Well," he said, "the clock is running, so let's get started, shall we?" He peered over the top of his thick glasses. "I know we've been over this before, but refresh my memory, will you? Mr. Shepherd...when exactly did you begin having these delusions that you were a dog?"

A final thought...

Our nine-year-old "grafted in" grandson Benji has gotten the bug to write. He has heard me tell him stories for his entire life, and now he is beginning to write his own stories of things he studies about in school and other things he is interested in. I won't vouch for the accuracy of this little history on "Cristofer" Columbus, but it shows imagination and out-of-the-box thinking. Way out of the box. I'd like to think I may have influenced a future author.

This made me laugh. I hope it will do the same for you.

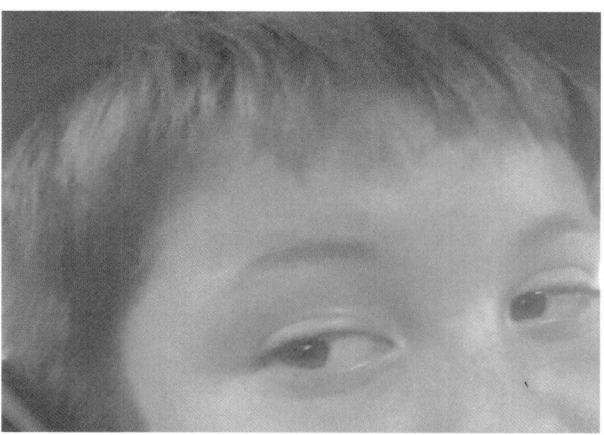

Turkey Survival with Cristofer Columbus

(Cristofer Columbus Is Not A Turkey. He Is an Early Explorer)

Once upon a time there was a turkey named Cristofer Columbus. He had 7 brothers and 5 sisters. His mom was 73 his dad was 99. His age was 16, and his age in human years is about 2 years old. He was on a mission to find out how to survive Thanksgiving and get on the Santa Maria and go to what he thought was India, but he went to the Bahamas near North America. Then I came in, and I asked him what his name was, and he responded like this: "Your mama looks like a frog, and I am not going to her house!" Then I said, "Are you drunk, 'cause you look like you have a screw loose in your head." He replied, "O you're saying what's my name? My name is Cristofer Columbus." I said, "My name is Benjamin Shaw I am just 9 years old and somehow I got on the Santa Maria from time traveling. I had just come from school with my favorite teacher, Ms. Katy Scott. "Then I realized we had learned about Cristofer Columbus. So, I jumped back in a portal and I told Ms. Katy what happened, and she did not believe me so, I showed her the portal that I found, and she was amazed. We said by, and then I turned into a turkey. So, I flew in the portal, and then I ran for my life from the crew members. I finally found Cristofer and then I asked him "What happened to me?"

The next day Cristofer Columbus and I had an argument where we broke up to go on our own. I also turned back in to a human. After that we got off the boat. So, I said "I am happy we haven't met again. Then I saw a platoon of Indians called the Tinos. So, I went to them and said "Do you guys know Cristofer Columbus. They said something I could not understand like g. So, I just left them in San Salvador. Then I went back to Cristofer and we got along. Then I said, "Sorry for the other day." Then he said, "Yep sorry too." So, we went to Virginia and sat on the coast. Then we got tired of that and we time traveled to New York. Then we met Alexander Hamilton and George Washington. Then we went to the British then they tried to kill us.

Then we time traveled to Columbus's time. Then I went to Portugal and Spain. After that I went to my time and told my mom what happened. Then me and Columbus lived happily ever after.